T0272548

FIVE BANNERS

JOHN
FEINSTEIN

FIVE
BANNERS

INSIDE *the*
DUKE BASKETBALL
DYNASTY

....

Duke University Press   *Durham and London*   2024

Printed in the United States of America on acid-free paper ∞
Project Editor: Ihsan Taylor
Designed by Courtney Leigh Richardson
Typeset in Garamond Premier Pro and Knockout
by Copperline Book Services

Library of Congress Cataloging-in-Publication Data
Names: Feinstein, John, author.
Title: Five banners : inside the Duke basketball dynasty /
John Feinstein.
Other titles: Inside the Duke basketball dynasty.
Description: Durham : Duke University Press, 2024. |
Includes index.
Identifiers: LCCN 2024008005 (print)
LCCN 2024008006 (ebook)
ISBN 9781478026716 (hardcover)
ISBN 9781478059950 (ebook)
Subjects: LCSH: Duke Blue Devils (Basketball team)—History. |
Duke University—Basketball—History. | NCAA Basketball
Tournament. | BISAC: SPORTS & RECREATION / Basketball |
SPORTS & RECREATION / Coaching / Basketball
Classification: LCC GV885.43.D85 F456 2024 (print) |
LCC GV885.43.D85 (ebook) |
DDC 796.323/6309756563—dc23/eng/20240227
LC record available at https://lccn.loc.gov/2024008005
LC ebook record available at https://lccn.loc.gov/2024008006

Cover art: Duke's Christian Laettner releases his game-winning shot
against Kentucky as the clock expires in overtime of the NCAA East
Regional finals in the Spectrum in Philadelphia, March 28, 1992.
(Photo by Chuck Liddy/The Herald-Sun)

FOR THE DUKE BASKETBALL CLASS OF 1986,
THE CLASS THAT HAD FAITH IN
MIKE KRZYZEWSKI BEFORE, AS HE PUT IT,

"there was reason to have faith in me"

....

Contents

Acknowledgments

I want to thank, first and foremost, my agent, Andrew Blauner, and Duke University Press director Dean Smith (no, not that Dean Smith) for coming up with the idea to have me write a book about Duke Basketball to celebrate the school's 100th anniversary. I can honestly say it was a joy ride.

I'd also like to thank Mike Krzyzewski, not only for winning those five titles but also for helping me track down many of the key players from his teams. Of course, the really hard work was done by his executive assistant, Gerry Brown, who gathered the contact information and passed it on to me. I'm very grateful to both of them.

Getting the players to respond to my various emails and texts was the critical next step, and most were quite willing to talk. I knew most of the older ones—heck, I've known Grant Hill since he was sixteen—and their memories were quite vivid. I suspect that many of the younger players had no clue who I was, but they still responded when I dropped Coach K's name. I only wish that tactic worked as well with my children.

Being a long-ago (1977) Duke graduate helped me appreciate how remarkable Krzyzewski's forty-two-year run truly was in the pantheon of college basketball. During my undergraduate years, Duke was 50–56 overall and 9–42 in Atlantic Coast Conference (ACC) play. Once Mike got the program going, there were few winters in which he didn't win ten or more conference games—not to mention making the NCAA Tournament thirty-eight times in his last thirty-nine full seasons (there was no tournament in 2020 because of COVID-19) and reaching thirteen Final Fours, five of which ended with hanging a banner.

Thanks, as always, to family and friends—notably my longtime pal Keith Drum, who is very much a part of this book; and my three children, Danny, Brigid, and Jane, all of whom have heard more about Duke Basketball in their lives than you can possibly imagine.

—*John Feinstein*

DUKE UNIVERSITY PRESS wishes to recognize the life and accomplishments of photojournalist Chuck Liddy (1954–2024). Thank you for being a champion.

Introduction

It was basketball that first brought me to Duke University fifty years ago. It is basketball that still brings me back.

When I visited Duke as a high school senior in February 1973, my dad and I went to see Duke play second-ranked Maryland in Cameron Indoor Stadium. Duke wasn't very good—the team was en route to a 12–14 record—but that day the Blue Devils played superbly. Senior guard Gary Melchionni scored 39 points, and Duke pulled the upset. The building rocked with noise, and in the final minutes the Duke students sang the "Amen Chorus," which had become Maryland's end-of-game victory song.

As we left the building, I turned to my dad, who desperately wanted me to go to Yale—he was an adjunct faculty member there at the time—and said, "Dad, I'm sorry, but if I get in here, I'm going here."

I got in. I'm not sure my dad ever completely forgave me.

Never, though, did I imagine the ride that Duke Basketball would take me on when I made the decision to become a Duke student. Ten days after I arrived as a freshman in the fall of 1973, the men's basketball team had no coach. Bucky Waters, who had already been told his contract would not be renewed after his fifth season, resigned to become a fundraiser for the Duke hospital.

Athletic Director Carl James attempted to hire Adolph Rupp—yes, Adolph Rupp, the legendary University of Kentucky coach who had been forced into retirement by the school in 1972 because he had made the mistake of turning seventy. Rupp had won four national championships, the last one in 1958. He had also coached in college basketball's most important and famous game: the 1966 NCAA championship game, when his all-white Kentucky team lost to a Texas Western team that started five Black players. Books were written and movies were made about that game. Rupp never reached another Final Four.

James scheduled a press conference for October 18, three days after the official start of basketball practice, to introduce Rupp. But Rupp's farm director died suddenly, and Rupp told James that he couldn't leave his farm. James instead promoted Neill McGeachy, Waters's number-one assistant, and gave him a one-year contract.

The Blue Devils went 10–16 that season, the worst record in school history, and James informed McGeachy that he wouldn't be asked back as coach only minutes after the historic "eight-points-in-17-seconds" loss to North Carolina in Chapel Hill. Somehow Duke, leading by eight points with those 17 seconds left—at a time when there was no three-point shot—managed to lose in overtime that Saturday afternoon to Dean Smith's vaunted Tar Heels.

Bill Foster was hired to rebuild the program—and he did. But it took him four years. My last three years as an undergrad, while I was covering the team for Duke's student newspaper, the *Chronicle*, Duke was 40–40 overall and 7–32 in ACC play (including three first-round losses in the ACC Tournament), meaning my four-year record was 50–56 and 9–42.

When I repeat those numbers to people today, they don't believe me. Duke won more than thirty games *fifteen* times during Mike Krzyzewski's forty-two years as coach. From 1984 until Krzyzewski's retirement in 2022, Duke failed to win at least twenty games on only three occasions.

Duke last in the ACC? People would say to me—get real.

Back then, it was very real.

In 1978, when I was a night police reporter at the *Washington Post*, Foster turned it around completely. Duke went 27–7, won the ACC Tournament for the first time since 1966, and reached the national championship game.

I had convinced George Solomon, the sports editor of the *Post*, to let me cover the Final Four in St. Louis *if* Duke got that far. As a result, I was sitting in Foster's Friday press conference the day before the Blue Devils were to play Notre Dame in the semifinals. Someone asked him how his team had gone from last in the ACC a year earlier to the Final Four.

Foster, who had one of the greatest dry senses of humor I've ever encountered, looked right at me and said, "Well, John Feinstein graduated."

Everyone in the massive interview room began looking around, wondering who the hell John Feinstein might be. Only Ken Denlinger, the *Washington Post*'s great sports columnist (who had given me the floor of his hotel room as a place to sleep), had any clue what I looked like. He was the entire list.

The real answer to the reporter's question was, of course, that Duke had added two superb freshmen, Gene Banks and Kenny Dennard, to a lineup that included junior guard Jim Spanarkel and sophomore center Mike Gminski, and *that* was the reason for the team's remarkable turnaround.

Duke beat Notre Dame 90–86 the next afternoon—in those blessed and long-gone days when the Final Four semifinals were played in the afternoon—and finally lost to Kentucky 94–88 in the championship game.

The only player who graduated from that team was walk-on guard Bruce Bell (now a judge in Kentucky), but all sorts of off-court issues prevented that group from reaching those heights again—although the 1980 team did reach the Elite Eight after beating Kentucky on Kentucky's home court in the Sweet Sixteen.

By then, Foster, feeling unappreciated, had left to become the coach at South Carolina. Athletic Director Tom Butters began a search for a successor that landed on an unknown coach named Mike Krzyzewski, who had just finished going 9–17 at Army in his fifth season at his alma mater.

It was Steve Vacendak, Butters's newly hired number-two man, who had brought Krzyzewski to Butters's attention. Vacendak had been a great player for Duke on two Final Four teams in the 1960s. While living in Annapolis, Maryland, he had gone to watch a Krzyzewski-coached Army team play archrival Navy.

"Because my high school coach was friends with Bob Knight, Mike let me hang out with his team all day," Vacendak said. "I was blown away. He wasn't yet thirty and yet he sounded to me like a guy who'd been doing it for twenty years when he talked to his players. And his team could really guard."

Which is why Vacendak brought Krzyzewski up to Butters, who had told him he wanted someone who could really coach defense.

Butters had never heard the name. "What was his record this season?" he asked.

"It was 9–17," Vacendak said.

"*What*?" Butters said. "Are you trying to get me fired?"

Vacendak finally talked Butters into giving Krzyzewski an interview. He was impressed enough to give him a second interview. And a third. Still, he couldn't pull the trigger.

"What are you thinking?" Vacendak said after the third interview.

"I'm thinking he's the next great coach," Butters said. "But how can I hire a guy who was just 9–17 at Army?"

"If he's the next great coach," Vacendak answered, "how can you *not* hire him?"

Butters paused a moment. Then he said, "Go out to the airport and bring him back."

Vacendak found Krzyzewski waiting in line for his flight back to New York. "You need to come back," he said. "Tom has one more question to ask."

"What the hell can he possibly ask me?" Krzyzewski said. "He's interviewed me *three* times!"

"Just trust me," Vacendak said.

When Krzyzewski walked into Butters's office again, still steaming, he repeated what he had said to Vacendak.

"There's one question I haven't asked you," Butters said.

"*What*?"

"Will you take the job?"

Krzyzewski calmed down quickly. "What?" he said again, in an entirely different tone. And then: "Of course I'll take the job."

The rest is history—complicated history, but history nonetheless.

I

....

THE LONG *and* WINDING ROAD TO THE FIRST BANNER

What is often forgotten is the role played by Bill Foster in the dynasty that Mike Krzyzewski built.

One person who hasn't forgotten is Krzyzewski himself. "He did a remarkable job here," Krzyzewski said. "When he took over, the program was really struggling. It isn't just that he rebuilt, but that his success carried over to our recruiting in those early days."

As I've mentioned, it took four years for Foster to turn Duke around. He built his team around one holdover from the Bucky Waters–Neill Mc-Geachy era—Tate Armstrong—and six players he recruited in those first three seasons: Jim Spanarkel, Mike Gminski, Gene Banks, Kenny Dennard, and transfer point guards John Harrell and Bob Bender. They were the core of the 1978 team that played in the NCAA title game one year after finishing last in the ACC.

"When Coach K started recruiting me, the only reason I knew Duke was that '78 team," said Mark Alarie, the second-leading scorer on the 1986 team—Krzyzewski's first Final Four team. "I remembered liking those guys and rooting for them. If not for them, I wouldn't have had any idea what or who Duke was."

Alarie was part of the 1982 recruiting class, along with Johnny Dawkins, Jay Bilas, David Henderson, and Weldon Williams. This "class that saved Coach K" turned Duke from a team that went 38–47 in Krzyzewski's first three seasons into one that went 83–21 the next three seasons and played for the 1986 national championship.

"There's no doubt that ultimately the reason each of us chose Duke was Coach K," Bilas said. "But what that '78 team did and our memories of that team certainly helped get him in our doors."

Duke took off the year after the '82 class enrolled when point guard Tommy Amaker arrived and became a starter from his first game until his last in 1987. Remarkably, four of the '86 Final Four team's five starters are still involved in basketball: Amaker is the coach at Harvard; Dawkins is the coach at Central Florida; Henderson, once the coach at Delaware, is now a scout for the Cleveland Cavaliers; and Bilas is ESPN's top college analyst.

It wasn't an easy turnaround by any means. The 1982–83 team was deeply divided; the seniors, the last group recruited by Foster, knew the freshmen were more talented than they were but felt they had earned the right to play. By his own admission, Krzyzewski didn't handle a difficult situation well. By mid-February, Duke was a broken team: the seniors were angry at the freshmen, the freshmen were angry at the seniors, and the coach was flat-out mad.

Krzyzewski started the three seniors—Mike Tissaw, Chip Engelland, and Tommy Emma—on Senior Day against North Carolina. The first time Duke got the ball, Tissaw, whose range was (generously) out to five feet, fired an eighteen-foot jumper that came nowhere close. That was a harbinger of the entire day. North Carolina won 105–81, which left the Blue Devils with a 3–11 conference record and 11–16 overall.

Unfortunately, the season wasn't over.

In the first round of the ACC Tournament the next week in Atlanta, Duke faced Virginia and national player of the year Ralph Sampson. The game was competitive for a half, largely because Sampson committed two quick fouls and went to the bench. Virginia led 50–41 at halftime. The last 20 minutes were a nightmare for Duke. Virginia won the game 109–66, the worst loss of Krzyzewski's entire career—including his five years at Army.

That wasn't on Krzyzewski's mind after the game, when he and several friends went to a Denny's on the Atlanta Perimeter for a 2:00 a.m. breakfast/venting session. I happened to be present, and I've often told the story about that gathering and its significance.

Tom Mickle, Duke's sports information director, raised a water glass and proposed a toast to "forgetting tonight."

Krzyzewski raised his glass and said, "Here's to never f—ing forgetting tonight."

Krzyzewski was angry: angry with the Duke boosters he knew were in the hotel lobby screaming at Tom Butters to fire him; angry with Virginia coach Terry Holland for claiming Jay Bilas had been "trying to hurt Sampson"; angry with his players for giving up; but most of all, angry with himself for not doing a better coaching job.

Bilas laughed when he heard what Holland had said. "I wasn't trying to hurt anyone," he said. "I was trying not to get humiliated. And I failed miserably."

Krzyzewski never found anything about that game or evening funny. "It was actually an important night for me," he said. "I had to face up to the fact that I hadn't done a good enough job. I had to look at myself first and foremost. Sitting in that Denny's, it really hit me that, as angry as I was at others, it all came back to me eventually."

As a freshman (plebe) at West Point, Krzyzewski had learned that one of three answers was allowed when you were spoken to by an upperclassman: "Yes sir," "No sir," or—most important—"No excuse sir." That became his mantra in all things—especially his coaching—from that day forward. He never once publicly threw his players under the bus after a loss. The loss happened because he didn't coach well enough, or because the other team and the other coach were better.

. . . .

The loss to Virginia on what became known as the "night at the Denny's" proved to be Krzyzewski's nadir. The next season, with Amaker added to Dawkins, Alarie, Bilas, and Henderson, Duke became a good team again. In their ACC opener at Virginia, the Blue Devils beat the Cavaliers 78–72, ending their nine-game losing streak to UVA. Even with Sampson gone, Virginia was still very good—good enough to make that year's Final Four. The victory in University Hall was the start of a sixteen-game Duke winning streak against Holland's teams.

Even so, after a 14–1 start, there were tough times. Duke lost at home to fifth-ranked Maryland and on the road (badly) to No. 12 Wake Forest. That brought North Carolina, top-ranked and unbeaten, into Cameron Indoor Stadium. The Tar Heels were led by Michael Jordan, Sam Perkins, and Kenny Smith. That game turned out to be a turning point in the Duke-Carolina rivalry in ways Krzyzewski didn't clearly understand until years later.

Much of the focus that night was on the Duke student section, the so-called Cameron Crazies, who had gone way over the line a week earlier in taunting Maryland's Herman Veal, who had been accused of sexual assault. After the media had excoriated the students for their behavior, school president Terry Sanford wrote a letter to the student body, which ran on the front page of the *Chronicle*. "We're better than this," he told the students, and he encouraged them to be funny, be clever, and support the team but not to go over the invisible line they'd clearly crossed the previous Saturday.

The students came through. They showed up wearing halos, and when North Carolina took the court, they held up signs that said, "Welcome honored guests." Shortly before tip-off, the Blue Devil mascot delivered a dozen roses to Dean Smith—who wasn't amused even a little bit.

When the students didn't like an official's call, they chanted "we beg to differ" instead of the traditionally obnoxious profane chant most student bodies prefer. And when a Tar Heel was shooting free throws, instead of waving their arms, they held up signs that said, "Please miss."

In all, a brilliant performance.

Their team was also pretty good, pushing UNC until the final buzzer. Smith, always uptight in Cameron, got into an argument with the scorer's table at one point, and Krzyzewski was just as furious when Smith didn't receive a technical foul after the incident. With seconds left and Carolina finally in control—it would win the game 78–73—Krzyzewski called a time-out for the express purpose of getting teed up himself.

"I told him [referee Mike Moser], I know you won't tee Dean up, so tee me up," Krzyzewski said later. "I told him my team deserved to win, and he and the other two guys had taken it away from them."

To be fair, Jordan and Perkins were a lot more responsible than the officials for taking the game away.

Both coaches were steaming after the game. When Smith was asked what he thought of the students' performance, he waved a hand and said, "I pay no attention to them. The schedule says we have to come over here and play them once a year. We do that, try to win the game like we did tonight, and go back to Chapel Hill."

Walking out, Smith passed a reporter who happened to be a Duke graduate (me) and stopped for a moment. "*You* think they're funny," he said angrily.

"I'm sorry, Dean," I answered. "Tonight, they *were* funny."

Krzyzewski had no issues with the students. The officials were another story. "There's a double standard in this conference," he said. "One for Dean Smith and one for the rest of us." That comment caused an uproar, especially in the decidedly biased North Carolina media. I decided to see what the other six ACC coaches might think. Four weren't going to touch the question, but Maryland's Lefty Driesell and Clemson's Bill Foster both backed Krzyzewski.

How much did that bother Smith? He called me, and his first comment was, "Did Mike tell you to write that story?"

"What do you think I'd have done," I asked, "if all the coaches said Mike was out of his mind?"

That calmed Smith down, but he still vented for a few more minutes. I wasn't the first reporter he had called after that game. Keith Drum, then the sports editor of the *Durham Morning Herald*, had written that *both* coaches were wrong—Smith should have been teed up at least once and that Jordan and Perkins had been responsible for Duke's loss, not the referees.

Both coaches rewarded Drum with angry phone calls. "I guess I wrote a pretty good column," he said, laughing at the memory.

That night was the beginning of years of tension between Smith and Krzyzewski. It also signaled the beginning of Duke's parity in the rivalry with North Carolina. In the next two UNC games that season, the Blue Devils lost in double overtime in Carmichael Auditorium and then, a week later, beat the Tar Heels in the semifinals of the ACC Tournament.

After the game in Carmichael, Drum wrote that "the best team in Carmichael Auditorium on Saturday was not the winning team." Smith didn't bother calling him this time. But after Duke's 77–75 win in Greensboro, he spotted Drum and me walking past his team's locker room minutes after the game had ended. He put out his postgame cigarette, walked across the hall, and said to Drum, "Congratulations. You must be very proud of *your* team."

Drum had gone to UNC.

....

Five days after the "double-standard" game, North Carolina State, the previous year's national champion, came to Cameron. This time, the students did not have a good night.

The Wolfpack had graduated Sidney Lowe, Dereck Whittenburg, and Thurl Bailey off their championship team and were now led by junior Lorenzo Charles, the hero of the national championship game the previous spring; his dunk at the buzzer had provided the margin in NC State's 54–52 victory. Unfortunately, Charles had been involved in an embarrassing offseason incident in which he and a couple of friends had robbed a Domino's pizza deliveryman. No money was stolen, just pizzas. When the incident became public, there was no way the Duke students were going to let Charles out of Cameron without hearing from them.

First, they had twenty Domino's pizzas delivered to NC State coach Jim Valvano a few minutes before tip-off. Valvano enjoyed the students as much as Smith despised them. He paid for the pizzas and then handed them out to the students sitting behind the State bench.

"I always thought I'd be the perfect coach for the Duke students," Valvano said once upon a time. "They were funny and I love funny. We'd have been a good match."

During player introductions, when Charles was introduced, the students sailed empty Domino's boxes onto the court. Charles was not amused.

"I looked him in the eye when we lined up for tip-off," Alarie said. "I could see by the look on his face that we were in trouble. If there was ever a case where the students should have let a sleeping dog lie, that was it."

Charles scored 34 points and had 14 rebounds, and NC State won 79–76, with Charles making the key plays down the stretch.

"If I'd had three game balls, I'd have given one to Lo [Charles], one to Domino's, and one to the students," Valvano said later. "No doubt they helped us win that game."

The loss was Duke's fourth in a row—all to good teams.

Once again, the critics were in full voice. Starting 14–1 against a weak schedule was nice, but four losses in a row to conference rivals was more proof that Krzyzewski was in over his head.

"We kept hearing Coach K was going to be fired at the end of the season," Bilas said. "That bothered us. We'd come to Duke to play for *him*. We were wondering if we were going to have to transfer."

Tom Butters was aware of all the problems—the carping from the boosters and the media, the doubts he knew the players must be having, and the doubts Krzyzewski was probably having about his future. He was in his office early on Friday morning, January 27. He knew Krzyzewski wouldn't be in until midmorning because he made a habit of staying up very late looking at tape with his coaches after games—win or lose. Butters left word in the basketball office for Krzyzewski to please come see him when he got in.

"That was unusual for me," Butters said. "I usually met with my coaches in their offices, so I knew the message would make Mike a little nervous, but I wanted to see him as soon as he got in because the team was leaving that afternoon to go to Clemson."

Krzyzewski arrived in Butters's office shortly after 10:00. "I was a little nervous," he said. "I didn't think he was going to fire me, but I wondered why he wanted to see me. I knew he wouldn't be any happier with four straight losses than I was."

Butters told Krzyzewski he was frustrated with what was going on in and around the basketball program. "I've got boosters screaming I need to change coaches; I've got media insisting I hired the wrong coach. None of that bothers me. But I've also got a coach who doesn't know how good he is and how much I believe in him."

He paused. "So, there's only one thing to do."

He pushed a pile of papers across the desk to Krzyzewski.

Krzyzewski stared at it for a moment, looked at Butters, and said, "This is a new contract."

Butters nodded. "It's for five years. No more doubts about your future or what I think of the job you're doing."

"I thought his eyes glistened a little bit," Butters said years later. "I think he was surprised that I'd think that was the time to extend him. But I was convinced it was the right thing to do."

Butters had to deal with angry threats from boosters in the aftermath of the announcement, but he never backed away from it.

Krzyzewski met with his team that afternoon before the bus trip to Clemson. He had never brought up his job status in the past. Now, he did.

"I know you guys have been hearing a lot of stuff about how long I'm going to be here," he said. "I also know you've been concerned. Well, you don't have to be concerned anymore. Mr. Butters just gave me a new five-year contract. I'm going to be here longer than any of you will be."

"It really was a relief," Alarie said. "We heard the rumors, we knew there were people who wanted him gone. Thing is, we never lost confidence in him. We wanted to play for him."

Coincidence or not, the Blue Devils got on a roll after that. They won at Clemson and at Georgia Tech on a Saturday–Monday trip; beat Virginia again; won *at* Maryland; and finally got a win over Wake Forest, blowing a big lead in Cameron before Alarie hit a fifteen-foot jump shot to win the game in overtime.

They ended the ACC regular season at 7–7, tied for third in the conference with Wake Forest—after the 1–4 start—and with an overall record of 22–8. In the first round of the ACC Tournament, they won another overtime game, beating Georgia Tech on an Amaker jumper in what amounted to an NCAA play-in game: winner goes, loser stays home.

A day later, they finally climbed the Carolina mountain, hanging on for dear life in a 77–75 victory. Prior to that victory, Krzyzewski had told his players he wanted no celebrating after the game. "We're the better team," he said. "When we win, we line up, shake hands, and head for the locker room. That's it."

When the buzzer went off, Bilas did what he was told. He turned and headed for the handshake line. "Then I looked up and saw Coach K at midcourt hugging Johnny [Dawkins]. I thought, 'What the hell is this?'"

Krzyzewski laughed at the memory. "Yeah, I kind of lost it," he said.

"We'd been so close twice that season and we finally got them. It ended up being a lesson for me: never celebrate until you're done."

The next day, emotionally drained, Duke lost the championship game to Maryland. Lesson learned. Most Duke fans weren't that upset about the Maryland loss. They had bumper stickers made up that said, "Duke–77, North Carolina–75. . . . March 10, 1984."

"I didn't like that," Krzyzewski said. "The goal is to beat everyone, not just one team."

There was no doubt, however, that beating that one team was a big deal. A very big deal.

....

The tournament win over Carolina was Duke's last of the season. Returning to the NCAA Tournament for the first time since Bill Foster's farewell season in 1980, the Blue Devils were sent to Pullman, Washington, as a No. 3 seed in the West Regional. Their second-round opponent (the top four seeds in each regional had a bye in the first round) was No. 6 seed Washington. This was before the NCAA began "protecting" higher-seeded teams by keeping them close to home or at least away from sites where the lower-seeded team was much closer to home.

Pullman is 285 miles from Washington's Seattle campus. It is 2,632 miles from Duke's Durham campus. Washington won the game 80–78. It ended with Amaker throwing an alley-oop pass to Dawkins, who appeared to get undercut as he went up to catch the ball. There was no whistle.

"Was I fouled?" Dawkins asked rhetorically years later. "In today's game, it would have been two shots, the ball, and a possible ejection. Wasn't even close."

The no-call ended Duke's 1983–84 season with the team posting a 24–10 final record. The following year, all five starters would return. Krzyzewski's new contract, the NCAA bid, *and* the win over Carolina had quieted his doubters.

Picked second in the ACC—behind Georgia Tech—in preseason polls, the Blue Devils eventually finished fourth, losing at home to Carolina in the season finale with first place at stake. They had ended a nineteen-season losing streak in Chapel Hill earlier in the year but couldn't handle the pressure of playing for a regular-season championship, losing to the Tar Heels 78–68.

That win left UNC in a tie for first place at 9–5 with Georgia Tech and NC State. Duke and Maryland tied for fourth at 8–6. Duke beat Maryland in the first round of the ACC Tournament, but Alarie sprained an ankle and played little in Duke's loss to Georgia Tech the next day.

Once again, the Blue Devils were a No. 3 seed in the NCAAs and were sent to Houston to play Pepperdine in the first round of the Midwest Regional. This was the first year that the NCAA expanded the tournament to sixty-four teams, meaning that there were no byes and everyone played in the first round.

With Alarie playing but still hobbled, Duke beat Pepperdine, giving Krzyzewski his first NCAA Tournament win. Two nights later, Duke lost 84–83 to a very good Boston College team. This was the "Year of the Big East"—three Big East teams made the Final Four, and Villanova stunned Georgetown in the national championship game. If Boston College had not lost to Memphis at the buzzer in the round of 16, there could have been four Big East teams headed to Lexington, Kentucky, for the season's final weekend.

The loss to BC brought on a new complaint: Krzyzewski had recruited players good enough to make the NCAA Tournament but not good enough to make an impact in March.

The players heard. "We were going to have four seniors and me [a junior] starting the next season," Tommy Amaker said. "It was time to take that next step."

Which they did. Right from the beginning, the 1985–86 Blue Devils were clearly one of the class teams in the nation. They beat St. John's (coming off a Final Four appearance the previous spring) and Kansas to win the first preseason National Invitation Tournament (NIT) in Madison Square Garden, Duke's first championship in a national tournament in the program's history.

They reeled off sixteen straight wins to start the season and went to Chapel Hill to play top-ranked North Carolina ranked No. 3 nationally. The game was the first played in the newly minted Dean E. Smith Center, which was instantly known to every person on the planet not employed by the University of North Carolina as the "Dean Dome." The building was a $38 million, 21,000-seat palace for basketball. The game was played at an intensity level worthy of March. Krzyzewski was teed up twice in the first half by referee David Dodge, and UNC went on to win 95–92.

"We played well that day," Bilas said. "But no matter how well we played, there was no way we were winning in that building that afternoon."

Two days later, still emotionally drained, Duke lost at Georgia Tech. At one point during that season, UNC, Duke, and Georgia Tech were all ranked in the Top 3 nationally.

The Tech loss dropped Duke to 16–2. As it turned out, the Blue Devils would win their next twenty-one games. That streak, however, brought them one win short of their goal.

The Blue Devils beat North Carolina to win the ACC regular-season title in the home finale for Dawkins, Alarie, Bilas, Henderson, and Williams. Then they beat Georgia Tech 68–67 in the ACC Tournament championship game, and after winning a rocky first-round NCAA Tournament game against Mississippi Valley State, they cruised to the Final Four.

Duke had to play Navy in the East Regional final in the New Jersey Meadowlands. The Midshipmen were led by David Robinson and had beaten Syracuse—*at* Syracuse—on their way to the Elite Eight.

"I couldn't believe I was one step from my first Final Four and my team had to play Navy—*Navy*!" Krzyzewski said years later. "It was as if the basketball gods were playing some kind of a trick on me."

Prior to the game, Krzyzewski gave perhaps his most impassioned pregame talk. "Look guys, you can't possibly understand what that team down the hall has done to be here," he said. "I do understand, and I'm so damn proud of them I want to give them each a hug."

He paused. "But *they're* Navy and *I'm* Army. I do not lose to Navy; *we* do not lose to Navy. So let me make this clear: if you don't win this game, don't even come back in here because I will never speak to any of you again."

Hyperbole? Of course. But the players got the message.

"There was absolutely no way we were going to lose," Dawkins said. "We knew exactly what he was trying to tell us."

The final score was 70–51, and it could have been worse. There were two memorable moments in the game. The first was when Dawkins practically jumped over Navy point guard Doug Wojcik and dunked. "Stupidest thing I ever did on a basketball court was trying to stop him," Wojcik, now an assistant coach at Michigan State, said thirty-seven years later.

And the second moment, soon after that, was when the Duke students —in the highest section of the arena because that's where the NCAA put students—began chanting, "Abandon Ship!"

"We heard it," Robinson said. "They weren't wrong."

A week later, in Dallas, Duke beat Kansas in the Final Four semifinals, Alarie somehow holding Danny Manning to four points. But the game took a lot out of the Duke players, notably Alarie and David Henderson. Louisville won the championship game 72–69. Alarie and Henderson, who had both shot well over 50 percent in the team's first thirty-nine games, combined to shoot 9-of-26. The whole team, which had shot 51 percent for the season, shot 40 percent on the night.

And yet, the Blue Devils almost won. Dawkins was brilliant in his last college game, scoring 24 points, and Amaker had 11 points, seven assists, and seven steals.

There was also a critical call that went against Duke. With the Blue Devils leading 67–64 and a little more than two minutes left, Louisville point guard Milt Wagner drove the baseline. Bilas was there and the two collided.

Block? Charge?

"I thought I was there," Bilas said. "I've looked at the replay and I still thought I was there. But it didn't matter what I thought or what I think."

What mattered was that referee Pete Pavia thought it was a block. Instead of Wagner fouling out and Duke getting the ball with a three-point lead, Wagner stayed in the game and made two free throws to cut the margin to 67–66. Louisville then made the plays in the final minutes to win.

Krzyzewski has always blamed himself for the outcome. "It was my first Final Four, my first championship game," he said. "I should have found ways to get Mark [Alarie] and David [Henderson] more rest. I didn't adapt to the idea that I was coaching a tired team."

Several years later, when Pavia was dying of cancer, he held a golf tournament to raise money for cancer research in Rochester, New York. He asked Krzyzewski, a non-golfer, to be one of the celebrities at the event. Krzyzewski went.

. . . .

By making it to, though losing, the national championship game and finishing 37–3, Duke was in an entirely different place than it had been three years earlier.

Krzyzewski had proved he could recruit big-time players. In 1985, Duke and North Carolina had gone head-to-head to get DeMatha star Danny Ferry, who was considered the best player in that year's high school class. Ferry chose Duke—a rare loss for Dean Smith to *anyone* in recruiting.

"I loved North Carolina and Coach Smith," said Ferry, "but I also loved Coach K's intensity and his style of play." Ferry paused and smiled. "And I thought Johnny Dawkins was cool. I thought it would be really cool to play with him, even if it was just for a year."

With the senior class of '86 gone, most people figured Duke would drop back considerably. Amaker was the only returning starter, and Ferry, now a sophomore, had to go from being a part-time player to the focal point of the team's offense.

But Krzyzewski had proved by then he wasn't a one-year recruiting star. He had continued to bring in very good players every year after the '82 recruiting class. Ferry (1985) might have been the most significant, but players like Billy King and Kevin Strickland (both 1984) and Quin Snyder (1985) were ready to move into more prominent roles. And there was a trio of talented freshmen on the 1986–87 team: Alaa Abdelnaby, Robert Brickey, and Phil Henderson.

The Blue Devils were hardly a dominant team that season, but they were good enough to finish 9–5—third in the ACC behind unbeaten (14–0) North Carolina and 10–4 Clemson. One loss—surprise!—irked Krzyzewski more than any other: the North Carolina game in Cameron. Once again, the Tar Heels were loaded with great players—including Kenny Smith, J. R. Reid, Scott Williams, and Jeff Lebo—and came into Cameron 11–1. The game was tight throughout, and two close calls near the end swung the momentum to UNC. Both calls were made by veteran referee Paul Housman.

When Krzyzewski vehemently argued the second call, Housman said to him, "Mike, if I missed either one of those calls, I'll buy you a Coke for each one."

"I don't want a f—ing Coke," Krzyzewski answered. "I want to win the damn game."

He didn't. When it was over, Krzyzewski went straight to his office and cued up the two calls. He then called a manager in, handed him a note, and told him to take it to Housman.

"You owe me *two* f—ing Cokes," it read.

The Blue Devils reached the Sweet Sixteen, where they lost to an Indiana team that would go on to win the national championship, Bob Knight's last moment of real glory. Much was made of the Knight-Krzyzewski, teacher-pupil matchup prior to the game. Knight was gracious in the aftermath, talking about how well Duke had played and how proud he was of Krzyzewski.

"I'm not sure he would have been so gracious if we had won the game," Krzyzewski said later.

He would eventually learn the prescience of those words.

. . . .

As it turned out, 1987 was the only year between 1986 and 1992 that Duke failed to reach the Final Four. It was, however, a key bridge to Duke's subsequent success. After staying in the Top 20 all season and reaching the second weekend of the NCAA Tournament, Duke lost one starter—Amaker. Every other key player returned, and the 1987–88 Blue Devils were ranked in the Top 10 all season.

They beat North Carolina *three* times during that season, an unheard-of feat against the Dean Smith juggernaut. The third time was in the ACC title game, meaning that Duke had won the tournament twice in three years. They went into the NCAA Tournament as a No. 2 seed in the East Regional, then stunned top-ranked Temple in the regional final to reach the Final Four again.

They lost to Kansas in Kansas City in the semifinals, and when Kansas went on to beat Oklahoma in the championship game, it meant Duke had lost to the national champion three years in a row: Louisville, Indiana, and Kansas. By now, though, losing to the champion wasn't the goal; *being* the champion was the goal, and that wasn't going to be easy.

It wasn't as if North Carolina had taken a step back. The Tar Heels were still very formidable, and Smith, as competitive as anyone on the planet, wasn't about to back off from the challenge Krzyzewski was now providing.

"Watching those two during those years was a lot of fun," said Keith Drum, the longtime sports editor in Durham who went on to be an NBA scout for twenty-three years. "I was in college when Dean built his program, and he was easily the most intensely competitive person I'd ever met. Until I met Krzyzewski. He was right there with him."

With Danny Ferry and Quin Snyder back for their senior seasons—joined by the solid junior class of Phil Henderson, Alaa Abdelnaby, and Robert Brickey and two talented freshmen big men, Christian Laettner and Crawford Palmer—Duke was picked No. 1 in most preseason polls. The 1988–89 Blue Devils won their first thirteen games and were still ranked No. 1 when North Carolina came into Cameron and blew their doors off, 91–71. That was the season that Jim Valvano's North Carolina State career was first put in jeopardy by the early release of a book jacket accusing Valvano and his staff of numerous NCAA violations.

Bonded by the notion that the world was against them, the Wolfpack somehow won the ACC regular-season title. Duke ended up tied for second after winning the regular season finale in Chapel Hill.

But what might have been Duke's most important game had come a week earlier in a made-for-TV game against Arizona, played in the Meadowlands. The game was on NBC, agreed to by the two schools in order to showcase their national-player-of-the-year candidates, Duke's Ferry and Arizona's Sean Elliott.

Ferry won the statistical battle, scoring 29 points to Elliott's 24, but Arizona won the game. Duke rallied from an early 18-point deficit to lead by eight before Arizona rallied to take the lead 73–70 on an Elliott three-pointer.

With Arizona leading 77–75 and eight seconds left, the Wildcats' Anthony Cook missed a free throw. Duke grabbed the rebound, and Laettner drove the baseline at the other end and was fouled by Kenny Lofton with one second left. He needed to make both ends of a one-and-one to send the game to overtime, but his first shot hit the back rim, and Elliott rebounded as the clock went to zero.

Before anyone else moved, Krzyzewski went straight to Laettner and put a hand on his face. "You did *not* lose this game for us," he said, shouting up and into Laettner's ear. "You gave us a chance to win. You made a great play. That's what I want you to remember."

Krzyzewski and Laettner were directly in front of the NBC broadcast position, and commentator Al McGuire heard everything Krzyzewski said.

"That was one of the great coaching moves I've ever seen," McGuire said at dinner that night with broadcast partner Dick Enberg and me. "Moment like that, you lose a heartbreaking game like that, and he goes straight to the kid to make sure he understands it wasn't his fault."

McGuire paused for a moment and then said, "I guarantee you that kid will never miss a clutch shot again."

As usual, McGuire was right.

. . . .

Duke and North Carolina played in the ACC Tournament championship game for a second straight season, this time in Atlanta's Omni.

Duke had won the ACC title two of the previous three seasons. North Carolina hadn't won the tournament since its national championship season in 1982. That ratcheted up the stakes even beyond the normal Duke–North Carolina level of intensity.

Krzyzewski and Smith got into a shouting match during the first half, each coach suggesting the other limit conversations to his own players. At one point, Smith, the master of the never-let-'em-see-you-sweat coaching style, turned and kicked the scorer's table in frustration.

Carolina won the game 77–74 when Ferry's shot from half-court went in and out at the buzzer.

"If that shot had gone in, I don't know if the old coach would have been around for overtime," Smith said, another admission that the game was a big deal.

Both teams, having finished behind NC State in the ACC regular season, were selected as No. 2 seeds for the NCAA Tournament.

Smith, however, was furious that his North Carolina team—after beating Duke for the ACC title and winning two of their three matchups—was sent to the Southeast Regional, with first- and second-round games in Atlanta followed by a Sweet Sixteen in Lexington, Kentucky, while Duke was sent to a first and second round in Greensboro and a regional in its home away from home, the New Jersey Meadowlands. Although the committee members later insisted their thinking was that UNC deserved to not be in the same region with Georgetown, which was informally the tournament's top seed, and would have a better chance to reach the Final Four in a region where Oklahoma was the top seed, Smith wasn't buying it.

"Tom Butters was on the committee," he said later. "Where do you think he wanted his school to go?"

It turned out that both Smith and the committee were right. Oklahoma was upset in the round of 16 by Virginia. That didn't do North Carolina any good, though, because the Tar Heels lost in the same round to Michigan—which would go on to win the national championship.

In the meantime, Duke got to play 11th-seeded Minnesota in the Meadowlands in the round of 16. Duke played Minnesota after escaping a difficult second-round game against West Virginia. Because UNC played a late game Friday and Duke played early, Smith knew that Duke had advanced after his team's loss to Michigan. When Smith's local beat writers—as was tradition—went to thank him after his last press conference of the season, his parting comment was, "I wish we could have played Minnesota."

Duke *did*, however, have to play top-seeded Georgetown in the regional final to get to the 1989 Final Four. The Blue Devils beat the Hoyas 85–77, with Laettner outplaying Georgetown's far-more-glorified freshman, Alonzo Mourning. That game turned out to be Laettner's coming-out party as a star. He scored 24 points and added nine rebounds and four assists. Mourning had 11 points, five rebounds, and zero assists. Laettner made nine of his ten shots from the field, none of them three-point attempts because he hadn't developed a three-point shot yet. In fact, he attempted only one three-pointer all season—and made it.

The victory was an emotional one for Krzyzewski because Quin Snyder did a remarkable job running the offense against Georgetown's pressure defense. Krzyzewski had always been very close to his point guards, starting with Tommy Amaker, who was the catalyst on his first Final Four team in 1986. Snyder's career had been up-and-down for most of four years, but he had taken firm control of the team as a junior in 1987–88 and, along with Ferry, was the team's co-captain his senior season.

Facing the Georgetown pressure for 40 minutes, Snyder had seven assists and one turnover and successfully got the ball into the hands of Laettner, Henderson (23 points), and Ferry (21 points).

When Krzyzewski was asked about Snyder's play in the postgame interview on CBS, he burst into tears. "I just knew what it meant to Quin to play so well and to get to end his career in Seattle."

Snyder had grown up in the Seattle suburb of Mercer Island, and with the Final Four being played in the Kingdome, Duke's victory meant he would play his final college game in his hometown.

Unfortunately, the homecoming didn't turn out well. Duke jumped out to a 26–8 lead against Seton Hall in the semifinals, but Robert Brickey went down with a knee injury on a drive to the basket and Duke's momentum stalled completely. Brickey had become a key player that season—especially at the defensive end of the court—but his absence could only partly explain the game's complete turnaround.

In the final 29 minutes, the Pirates outscored the Blue Devils by an astonishing margin of 87–52 to win 95–78. Ferry was heroic in his last college game, scoring 34 points and grabbing 10 rebounds, but it wasn't nearly enough.

The good news for the Blue Devils was that it had reached three Final Fours in four seasons. The bad news was that they still had yet to win one.

. . . .

With Ferry and Snyder gone, the 1989–1990 team would be young at two key positions: center and point guard. Laettner, who had averaged 8.9 points as a freshman, would have to become a big-time scorer; the three seniors—Abdelnaby, Henderson, and Brickey—would have to go from being complementary players to key players; and the point guard would be a freshman, Bobby Hurley.

As with Tommy Amaker in 1983, Krzyzewski simply handed Hurley the ball and said, "You're it." There were two other highly recruited guards on the team—Billy McCaffrey and Thomas Hill—but neither was a point guard, and both had the luxury of coming off the bench to spell more-experienced players.

Only two players started all thirty-eight games during the season: Laettner and Hurley. McCaffrey and Hill combined to play about 28 minutes a game as they grew into being ACC players. Hurley played more minutes than anyone on the team, averaging 34 a night. Talk about learning on the job.

"I always had a lot of confidence in myself, and I had played on really good teams in high school," Hurley said. "But there were nights when I felt I was in over my head. It wasn't an easy year."

The Blue Devils were still very good, even though every one of their players was in a new role. They finished second in the ACC regular season behind Clemson with a 9–5 regular-season record—one game behind the Tigers and one ahead of Georgia Tech and North Carolina. The presence of the Tigers at the top of the regular-season standings was unusual, to say the least. Clemson had been an original conference member in 1954. Prior to the 1989–90 season, it had won a total of *zero* conference championships, regular season or tournament.

Clemson's presence atop the standings caused a fair amount of speculation in the national media that the ACC was having a down year. Late in February, Clemson coach Cliff Ellis responded to that idea.

"The reason the media thinks the ACC is having a down year is because Clemson's in first place," he said. "If Duke or North Carolina was in first place, no one would be saying the league was down."

Duke actually could have tied the Tigers for first place if it had been able to win the regular-season finale in Cameron against North Carolina; but, just as in 1985, the Blue Devils made a mess of Senior Day, losing to the Tar Heels 97–85. That left them alone in second place.

A week later, they were soundly beaten in the ACC semifinals by Georgia Tech, which was the hottest team in the league. With freshman point guard Kenny Anderson finding a comfort level and Dennis Scott and Brian Oliver becoming stars, the Yellow Jackets became known in the media as "Lethal Weapon 3."

Georgia Tech beat Virginia—which had upset both North Carolina and Clemson—in the tournament final and was sent to the Southeast Regional as a No. 4 seed. North Carolina was sent to the Midwest Regional as a No. 8 seed, its lowest seed since the NCAA had started seeding teams in 1979. Carolina was 19–13, the first time since 1966 that the Tar Heels had double-digit losses.

Duke and Clemson were both sent to the East Regional, Duke as a No. 3 seed and Clemson as a No. 5 seed—even though the two teams had split their regular-season meetings, Clemson had finished one game ahead of Duke in the ACC standings, and both had lost in the ACC semifinals. Maybe Cliff Ellis wasn't being paranoid when he talked about the perception that most people thought something was wrong in the ACC because Clemson was in first place.

North Carolina made it to the Sweet Sixteen for a tenth straight season, upsetting top-seeded Oklahoma 89–87 on a buzzer-beating shot by Rick Fox. Arkansas then crushed the Tar Heels 96–73 in the regional semifinals.

Georgia Tech had to survive two very difficult games in the Southeast Regional in New Orleans. They first beat Michigan State 81–80 in overtime, then they got past Minnesota 93–91—thanks in large part to Dennis Scott's 40 points—to reach the school's first ever Final Four.

But the most melodramatic of the regionals took place in the Meadowlands, which was hosting the East Regional for a fifth straight season.

Connecticut had been one of *the* stories in college basketball all season, coming from the lower echelon of the Big East in Jim Calhoun's fourth season as coach to win both the regular-season and tournament titles. That had earned them the No. 1 seed in the East, and they arrived in East Rutherford with a 30–5 record and the heavy favorite to advance to Denver and the Final Four.

Duke was lucky to be back in the Meadowlands for a fourth time in five seasons. The Blue Devils had to come from behind late in the second round to beat St. John's, and they found themselves facing seventh-seeded UCLA, which had upset second-seeded Kansas.

The fourth team in the regional was Clemson, almost an afterthought—except that the Tigers came within a whisker (pun not intended) of upsetting the Huskies. They rallied from 19 points down to take a 70–69 lead with one second to play. Connecticut had to go the length of the court to score to avoid its dream season coming to a very sudden end.

Calhoun had Scott Burrell, who was also a baseball pitcher, throw the inbounds pass. He tossed a strike in the corner to Tate George. With the Clemson players afraid to foul, George caught the pass and launched a shot as the buzzer sounded. It swished, and he was buried underneath his teammates.

There was no replay in those days, and the officials ruled the shot good right away. Almost thirty years later, Cliff Ellis wasn't so sure. "I still think if we'd had replay, the shot wouldn't have counted," he said. "It wasn't like he caught and flung. He caught, squared up, and shot."

Regardless, it counted, so instead of playing Clemson on Saturday, Duke played UConn after holding off UCLA 90–81. Very few people expected Hurley to be able to handle the Huskies' 94 feet of pressure defense.

Except he did. He shot the ball poorly—0-of-9 from the field—but he had eight assists and only two turnovers while playing 43 minutes.

The reason Hurley played 43 minutes was that the game went into overtime. Abdelnaby, playing eight miles from where he had gone to high school, had the game of his life—27 points and 14 rebounds—but he missed a short turnaround jumper that could have won the game in regulation.

UConn appeared to have control in overtime, up two with the ball in the final minute. But there was a 10-second difference between the shot clock and the game clock, and Duke elected to play defense rather than foul. With the shot clock about to go off, George badly missed a jumper from almost the same spot from which he had made his buzzer-beater against Clemson. Laettner rebounded with eight seconds to go and quickly pitched the ball to Hurley.

Always aggressive, Hurley charged across midcourt and saw Henderson with his arm up running along the left side.

"What I remember most about that game is how poorly I shot," Hurley said. "But that pass almost became my last memory of that season."

George saw the pass coming and, like a football cornerback, jumped the route and had the ball in his hands. But he never gained control, and with Krzyzewski frantically screaming for a traveling call, he bobbled the ball out-of-bounds in front of the Duke bench.

"He wasn't traveling because he never had the ball," Krzyzewski said later. "I just couldn't think of anything else to do."

Duke used its last time-out to try to calm things down and set up a play. There were 2.6 seconds left. Krzyzewski called a play for Abdelnaby to screen on the baseline for Henderson, who already had 21 points. Laettner was the inbounder.

But when the teams came out of the huddle, Krzyzewski noticed that Calhoun wasn't guarding Laettner, opting for an extra defender to clog the middle or get over a screen. He turned to Laettner and Brian Davis, who was standing near midcourt as a safety outlet, and yelled "special."

It was a short-clock play that involved two quick passes—one from Laettner to Davis, the other from Davis back to Laettner who, presumably, would step inbounds unguarded. The other three Duke players on the court—Hurley, Henderson, and Abdelnaby—didn't even know the play had been changed, which was probably a good thing since they carried out the play as if expecting the ball to go to Henderson.

Laettner made his inbounds pass to Davis, who fired it right back to him. Laettner took one dribble and, from just left of the foul line—about three feet from the exact spot where he had missed the free throw against Arizona thirteen months earlier—he made a quick fake so that the Huskies' Nadov Henefeld flew past him and then put up a shot. The ball was in the air as the buzzer sounded.

It swished, giving Duke an improbable 79–78 victory.

Al McGuire had been right. And not for the last time.

....

Laettner's shot and Duke's victory actually caused some problems for me. When the game ended, I walked onto the court, as media members were allowed to do in those days, to talk to players and coaches while the nets were coming down.

When I found Krzyzewski, I shook his hand and patted him on the back with my notebook in congratulations. Then we talked for a few minutes.

The next morning, I was doing *The Sports Reporters*, the longtime ESPN show that usually consisted of three writers and the great Dick Schaap as the host. For some reason, Joe Valerio, the show's producer, had asked Dick Stockton, who had done play-by-play on the Duke-Connecticut game, to be the third panelist along with Mike Lupica and me.

Somewhere in the midst of our discussion of the last play, Stockton suddenly said, "Well, what I noticed in the postgame celebration was John Feinstein hugging Mike Krzyzewski."

Here we went again with the "Duke guy" thing. I hadn't come close to hugging Krzyzewski, but there was Stockton accusing me of it on national TV.

Stockton and I never got along, but this was over the line. Fortunately, Joe Valerio had tape of the postgame celebration, which showed me patting Krzyzewski on the back.

"You probably hugged him later," Stockton said.

"You probably owe me an apology *now*," I said.

I didn't get one.

I have never publicly called Duke "we," and, if anything, at times I've been tougher on the school than it deserved. My good friend Mike Wilbon never calls Northwestern anything *but* "we," and everyone is fine with it. In fact, it's part of his TV schtick. Then again, he's now a TV guy 100 percent of the time. I'm not and have never wanted to be.

The victory over UConn put Duke into the Final Four for the fourth time in five seasons. It was also the least likely of Krzyzewski's Final Four teams—a team that had lost its last home game and been beaten soundly in the ACC Tournament. And yet, there they were, matching up in the first semifinal against Arkansas, while the University of Nevada, Las Vegas (UNLV) and Georgia Tech would play in the second game.

Once again, Hurley had to face a team whose calling card was pressure defense. In fact, Arkansas coach Nolan Richardson had labeled his team's style "40 Minutes of Hell."

To make things worse, Hurley woke up on the morning of the game sick, running a fever and unable to keep down any food.

"No way was I not playing," Hurley said. "But I felt pretty terrible."

He ended up playing 36 minutes, leaving the game twice to go to the locker room to be sick. The game was wild, both teams going on runs that seemed to put them in control. But Duke had the last run and pulled away to win 97–83.

"I guess it was just 30 minutes of hell," Hurley said when it was over, still white as a ghost, sitting in front of his locker.

The three seniors, finally becoming stars in their final moments playing for Duke, led the way: Henderson had 28 points; Abdelnaby, 21; and Brickey, 17. Laettner added 19 points and 14 rebounds. The game was seemingly played at Arkansas's pace—the Razorbacks averaged 95.3 points per game—but they were the ones who ran out of gas late.

The second game that afternoon was a classic: UNLV beat Georgia Tech 90–81, and what seemed apparent to those watching was that the two best teams in the tournament were facing one another in that second semifinal. Of course, that had appeared to be the case in the recent past: Houston and Louisville in 1983, before NC State beat Houston in the title game; Georgetown and St. John's in 1985, before Villanova shocked Georgetown two nights later; Duke and Kansas in 1986, before Louisville beat Duke to win the championship; and Oklahoma and Arizona in 1988, before Kansas stunned Oklahoma on Monday night.

What those four upsets had in common was this: the team that won the title played first on Saturday and had several hours of extra rest, and the team that won the second game was considered almost a lock to win on Monday night.

That was not, however, the case with Duke and UNLV.

"I think it might finally be Mike's time," *Philadelphia Daily News* basketball guru Dick "Hoops" Weiss said. "This isn't his best team, but it keeps finding a way to win."

Sadly for Krzyzewski and his team, Duke would run out of ways to win after the Arkansas victory. The Runnin' Rebels, talented as they were, did not take anything for granted. They had been to the Final Four twice previously under coach Jerry Tarkanian (1977 and 1987), but they had never been to the championship game. They'd already gotten two scares in the tournament: one from Ball State in the round of 16 (winning 69–67) and one from Georgia Tech. In between, they'd routed Loyola Marymount 131–101 in the regional final.

The Lions had become the darlings of the tournament after Hank Gathers, their star, died suddenly of a heart attack during the West Coast Conference Tournament. Even without Gathers, they'd humiliated defending champion Michigan (149–115) in the second round before beating Alabama to get to the regional final. But UNLV was too big, too strong, and too fast for them and overpowered them at their own game—run, run, and then run some more.

....

The Runnin' Rebels had been assembled by a shrewd and animated leader.

Jerry Tarkanian was, first and foremost, an elite coach. He won 784 games during his college coaching career at Long Beach State, UNLV, and Fresno State. The 1990 Final Four was the third of his UNLV tenure, and he would make it back a fourth time the following year. The Rebels had lost national semifinal games to North Carolina and Dean Smith in 1977 and to Indiana and Bob Knight in 1987. That meant that in his four Final Four appearances, Tarkanian coached against three Hall of Fame coaches—Smith,

Knight, and Krzyzewski. Additionally, in his first Elite Eight game while at Long Beach, his team had lost to UCLA and John Wooden 57–55.

And yet, Tarkanian's reputation was sullied by an ongoing feud with the NCAA dating to his Long Beach days, when he became the first successful coach to actively recruit junior-college players. Many cluck-clucked at this; one of his loudest critics was former NCAA executive director Walter Byers, who claimed, among other racist comments, that Tarkanian's teams played "a ghetto style of run-and-gun basketball with little attention to defense."

Byers wasn't just a racist; he just knew nothing about basketball. If you asked other coaches—including Krzyzewski—they would tell you that Tarkanian was a genius at the defensive end of the court. "I'm not sure anyone ever taught it better," Krzyzewski said. In 2013, with backing by Krzyzewski and Knight, Tarkanian joined them in the Hall of Fame.

What most infuriated the NCAA—other than Tarkanian's consistent success—was his refusal to play the "student-athlete" game. Once, when he was asked why he had so many transfers on his team, he said, "Their cars are already paid for."

Nowadays, of course, those cars would be legal.

Most famously, after an envelope containing $1,000 in cash fell out of an Emery Express envelope en route from the Kentucky basketball office to the father of a recruit, Tarkanian said, "The NCAA is so mad at Kentucky, it's going to give Cleveland State two more years of probation." The comment dated to a 1973 column that Tarkanian had written for the Long Beach local newspaper claiming the NCAA loved to pick on the little guys while turning a blind eye to violations committed by the big guys.

Ironically, Tarkanian had become one of the big guys at UNLV. His 1990 Final Four team was experienced and deep; Duke was experienced but not deep. Vegas was the much better team—and played that way right from the start of the championship game.

The Rebels led 47–35 at halftime, leaving some hope that Duke could rally. But any hope that might happen was wiped out early in the second half, when UNLV went on an 18–0 run to lead by 30.

It might have gotten worse, but with the job done, the Rebels took their foot off the gas and cruised to the title. The final score of 103–73 was the largest margin in an NCAA championship game, surpassing UCLA's 78–55 victory over North Carolina in 1968. No team has approached that margin since then.

"If I had a hat I would tip it to them," Krzyzewski said in his postgame press conference. "They beat us in every way possible."

Later that night, unable to sleep even with no game tape to watch, Krzyzewski sat in his hotel suite with his head buried in his hands. He was surrounded by friends and family, who were smart enough to say nothing and allow him to suffer in silence.

Krzyzewski's mother, Emily, walked into the room and saw her younger son with his head in his hands.

"Mike!" she said sharply.

For a moment, he didn't answer, convinced he was having some kind of dream—or nightmare.

"Mike!" she said again.

"Ma!" Krzyzewski said, looking up at his mother.

"You'll do better next year," she said. "Don't worry about it."

Krzyzewski shook his head. "Ma, you don't understand," he said. "We made it to the championship game. The only way to do better than that is to win the whole thing. Doing that is *really* hard."

"I know," Emily Krzyzewski said. "You'll do better next year."

She turned and walked out of the room.

2

....

BANNER ONE

The feeling in the aftermath of the UNLV disaster was that getting to the championship game had been a remarkable accomplishment for Duke, albeit with an awful final chapter.

The point guard, Bobby Hurley, was a freshman learning on the job; the three seniors—Alaa Abdelnaby, Robert Brickey, and Phil Henderson—had all had up-and-down college careers; and the one true star, Christian Laettner, was still only a sophomore.

"It was a classic glass-half-full, glass-half-empty situation," Mike Krzyzewski said. "I always preach 'next play, next game, next season' to the players whether we've done well or not done well. But the Vegas game was hard to put behind us."

No one felt that way more than Hurley. He had been sick the entire weekend, but he didn't see that as an excuse. "I was terrible in the Vegas game," he said. "It was humiliating. It took me a while to shake the memories of that night. It was a terrible feeling."

Abdelnaby, Brickey, and Henderson had finally become solid players as seniors, and their departure was noteworthy. The incoming freshman class included Marty Clark, a 6-foot-6 shooting guard from the Chicago suburb of Westchester, and Grant Hill.

Hill was 6-foot-8 and the son of Calvin Hill, a Yale graduate who had been an All-Pro running back for the Dallas Cowboys during a twelve-year NFL career. Grant Hill had no position because, for all intents and purposes, he could play four positions, from point guard to power forward. He had been the subject of an intense recruiting battle between Duke, North Carolina, and Georgetown.

"When I was young, I was a big Georgetown fan, since I lived in the D.C. area [Reston, Virginia] and they had great teams," Hill said. "I loved [Georgetown coach] John Thompson. But then I became a Carolina fan, and for a while that was where I wanted to go. But then I became a big Tommy Amaker fan when he got to Duke. He was from Northern Virginia just like I was, and I thought playing at the same place he played would be fun."

In the end, Hill chose Duke because of Amaker and Johnny Dawkins, another D.C.-area product, and because he liked Krzyzewski's intensity. He was an only child, and both of his parents—Calvin and Janet, a high-powered Washington businesswoman—were very involved in the decision.

"I think we both felt that if Grant turned out the way Amaker and Dawkins turned out, that would be a great thing," Calvin Hill said. "I honestly thought he'd end up at North Carolina, but after we visited Duke, everything changed."

Even after losing out on Hill, North Carolina had a superb recruiting class arriving in the fall of 1990 that included 7-foot center Eric Montross, 6-foot-10 forward Clifford Rozier, and guards Brian Reese and Derrick Phelps. That group, combined with returning players Rick Fox, King Rice, Pete Chilcutt, George Lynch, and Hubert Davis, made the Tar Heels the clear favorites in the Atlantic Coast Conference.

Duke, with one senior starter—Greg Koubek—was a year away from making another Final Four run, or so it appeared.

That notion felt accurate during the preconference schedule. The Blue Devils played in the preseason NIT and lost in the semifinals to Arkansas. The Razorbacks had returned all their key players from the team Duke had beaten in the previous year's Final Four and appeared to be ready for another outstanding season. The Blue Devils then lost to Georgetown in the ACC–Big East Challenge in a game that was played on Georgetown's home court. Neither loss was a disaster, and both were learning experiences for a young team. But when his team opened ACC play by getting clobbered 81–64 at Virginia, Krzyzewski threw one of his most famous temper tantrums.

The game in Charlottesville had started at noon, meaning that the team bus was back in Durham early, pulling into the Cameron Indoor Stadium parking lot shortly before five o'clock. The players were ready to return to their dorms for a quiet Saturday night.

Their coach had other ideas.

"Everybody, dressed, taped, and ready to go in fifteen minutes," Krzyzewski said. "You didn't show up for the game today, so now you'll show up for practice."

Nowadays, Krzyzewski wouldn't have been allowed to make his team practice on the same day as a game; NCAA rules dictate a team can't practice until the next calendar day after a game. That wasn't the case in January 1991.

"The message he was sending was simple," said Amaker, who was an assistant coach on that team. "The way we'd played against Virginia was unacceptable. And if they didn't like practicing right after playing a game, they had better show up to *play* the game."

The practice was intense and physical, and it culminated when Grant Hill broke his nose driving into a bevy of bodies to try to dunk the basketball. "The message we got from Coach K that day was clear," Hill said. "He wasn't so much angry that we'd lost a game, but angry at the way we lost. We had played soft, the other team was tougher than we were. If the other team was better, he could live with that. He wouldn't accept the other team being tougher. The good news was, we got the message. The bad news was, I ended up with a broken nose."

In a sense, Hill's broken nose symbolized the practice and the message Krzyzewski was trying to send. Four nights later, Duke beat Georgia Tech 98–57. The Yellow Jackets still had star point guard Kenny Anderson from the "Lethal Weapon 3" team that had gone to the Final Four a year earlier, but they looked helpless against the Blue Devils.

"After that game, I said to Mike that I thought this might be his best team," Tech head coach Bobby Cremins said. "They'd been to five Final Fours in six years [actually four in five years], but I thought it was his most complete team."

Impressive wins at Maryland and against Wake Forest followed, but the real coming out came exactly two weeks after the Virginia debacle. Fifth-ranked North Carolina came to Cameron with a 13–1 record, still very much the favorite to win the ACC.

The game was tight until the last five minutes, when Duke pulled away and ended up cruising to a 74–60 win. Carolina wasn't supposed to lose to *anyone* by a score like that, and Duke wasn't supposed to be ready to win that way against the Tar Heels.

"After that game, I think we began to understand how good we could be," Hurley said. "We certainly weren't intimidated by them, but they had beaten us twice the year before, so it was a big deal for us to beat them. Of course, it was always a big deal for us to beat them."

Naturally, the emotional win was followed by an emotional letdown—a loss at North Carolina State, which had lost its coach, Jim Valvano, after the 1990 season but still had Chris Corchiani, Rodney Monroe, and Tom Gugliotta on a team that would reach the NCAA Tournament.

After that game, Krzyzewski had assistant coach Pete Gaudet put together a tape specifically for Hurley. By then, there was no doubt about Hurley's ability to be an effective point guard in the ACC. He had improved his shooting and cut down on his tendency to force passes that led to turnovers. Hurley's temperament, however, was still an issue. There wasn't anybody in the building who didn't know when he was upset about something—whether it was with an official, an opponent, a teammate, or himself.

"I've always been an emotional player," Hurley said. "I just didn't realize how much my emotions were affecting the other guys. And when I got upset about a play or call, it often affected the next play or the one after that."

Gaudet was the staff's tape guru. He often put together tapes of opponents showing their strengths and weaknesses, both as a team and individually. Now, at Krzyzewski's request, he made a tape that only showed Hurley reacting badly to plays. It became known as "the whine tape."

"I was shocked when he showed it to me," Hurley said. "Imagine if a football quarterback let people see how upset he was all the time. I was the quarterback, and I was doing it—without a helmet to hide my face at all."

Hurley watched and learned. Not only did he begin to make a point of not letting people see his anger or frustration; he also began focusing more on the Krzyzewski "next play" mantra.

It made a difference in his play and in the play of his teammates.

"Seeing Bobby look and act more confident made us all more confident," Hill said. "Christian was our best player, but Bobby was the point guard. A coach can lead only so much; someone has to be the leader on the court. As the season wore on and we got better, Bobby became a much better leader."

Duke and North Carolina went into the regular season finale in Chapel Hill tied for the conference lead with 10–3 records. Carolina was ranked fourth in the country and Duke eighth. King Rice hit the game's first basket to give Carolina a 2–0 lead, but the Tar Heels never led again. The Blue Devils, with Laettner and Hurley each scoring 18 points, led by as many as 19 before Carolina put on one of its classic late rallies, closing the margin to three in the final minute. But Pete Chilcutt and Derrick Phelps each missed threes that could have tied the game, and Duke held on for an 83–77 victory.

No one had expected Duke to sweep the regular-season series with Carolina, much less win the regular-season title. "I had thought we could be a good team," Krzyzewski said. "By the end of the regular season, we were a very good team. The question was just how good we could become in March."

The early returns weren't encouraging. A week after Duke had beaten North Carolina in Chapel Hill, the teams played again, this time in the ACC championship game. Dean Smith always made a point of saying it was very hard to beat a good team three times in the same season—usually when his team was about to face a team it had already beaten twice.

This time, Duke was the team trying to beat an opponent three times, and it failed miserably. Carolina led from start to finish and won 96–74, a whipping so thorough that Krzyzewski benched his starters the last few minutes of the game.

Carolina's victory finally got the Tar Heels the spot they had wanted in the East Regional since the infamous "I wish we could have played Minnesota" draw in 1989. Carolina was seeded No. 1 in the East, meaning it would go to the Meadowlands for the regional. Duke was sent to the Midwest as the No. 2 seed behind top-seeded Ohio State.

As Krzyzewski walked to the team bus outside the Charlotte Coliseum, he wasn't thinking about where his team would be sent when the brackets were unveiled later that evening.

"I was trying to think about what to say to my team," he said. "They'd played so well during the season, and then they'd had one really bad day against a team that was on a mission."

Krzyzewski was always the last person to board the team bus. He would sit down in the front row across from the driver, and the bus would leave. This time, he got on the bus and told the driver to wait a minute. Then, instead of sitting down, he stood in front of his players.

"Fellas," he said. "If you play the way I know you can play, we're going to win the national championship."

With that, he sat down, and the bus pulled out.

"I'm not even sure I was really listening," Hurley said later. "I was so depressed about the way I'd played and the way we'd played, I was kind of lost in a fog. I remember hearing Coach K say 'we're going to win the national championship,' not in a pep-talk kind of way, but almost matter-of-factly. If it did nothing else, it got me thinking about what was to come, not what had just happened."

A little while later, the bus pulled off I-85 to stop at a restaurant so the coaches and players could watch the unveiling of the tournament brackets.

Most of the talk on the CBS broadcast was about one thing: could anyone beat undefeated, defending champion Nevada, Las Vegas, the same team that had humiliated Duke in the previous year's national title game?

The consensus among all the so-called experts was almost unanimous: no.

．．．．．．．．．．．．

The four number-one seeds from east to west were North Carolina, Arkansas, Ohio State, and UNLV.

Remarkably, UNC hadn't been to a Final Four since winning the national championship in 1982. Ohio State hadn't been to a Final Four since 1968. Arkansas and UNLV had both played in the 1990 Final Four, Arkansas losing to Duke in the semifinals and UNLV beating Georgia Tech and Duke to win its first national championship.

As it turned out, both Duke and North Carolina cruised to the Final Four in 1991, the first time the rivals had both gotten to the last weekend of the season.

The Tar Heels easily won two games in Syracuse and then played 12th-seeded Eastern Michigan in the regional semifinals after EMU had beaten both Mississippi State and Penn State. Carolina won 93–67 and advanced to Sunday afternoon's final against Temple, the region's No. 10 seed. Syracuse, the No. 2 seed, led by Derrick Coleman and Billy Owens, had become the first No. 2 seed to ever lose in the first round to a No. 15 seed when it was stunned by Richmond. The Owls then beat Richmond and followed up by beating Oklahoma State to reach the regional final in the Meadowlands for the second time in four years.

In 1988 the Owls had been the No. 1 seed, but freshman Mark Macon had been shut down by Duke's Billy King, and the Blue Devils beat them 73–63. Macon was now a senior, and he single-handedly kept his team in the game against Carolina, scoring 31 points. The Tar Heels led almost the entire game but had to hang on to win 75–72. The margin didn't matter to Dean Smith—going back to the Final Four did.

Two and a half hours after the nets came down in the Meadowlands, Duke cut down the nets in the Pontiac Silverdome.

The Blue Devils had stumbled early in their first-round game against Northeast Louisiana (now the University of Louisiana at Monroe) but had gotten on a roll after putting that game away in the second half. In the second round, they had beaten a good Iowa team by 15, and then in a rematch of the East Regional final of a year earlier, they beat Connecticut by 13; no last-second heroics were needed.

Two days later, in the finals against St. John's, the Blue Devils controlled the game from start to finish, leading 40–27 at halftime before winning

78–61. They had won four tournament games by an average margin of more than 21 points to get back to the Final Four, their fourth in a row and fifth in six years. This from a team that most people thought would be a year away from seriously contending for the national championship.

As the nets came down, Krzyzewski's wife, Mickie, stood to the side watching with a huge smile on her face. "Dean may be going to Indianapolis," she said. "But he's not going unaccompanied."

True. But the consensus on which team would cut down the final net hadn't changed: UNLV was 34–0 and had won only one game by less than double digits all season. The Rebels would play Duke in the second semifinal on Saturday after the teacher-pupil matchup between Dean Smith and Kansas coach Roy Williams in the opener.

There was a possibility of a Duke–North Carolina matchup in the finals, but almost no one expected it to happen.

As it turned out, it didn't.

....

As was his habit, Mike Krzyzewski didn't spend a lot of time celebrating his team's return to the Final Four. Almost from the minute the nets came down in Pontiac—which, for the record, is thirty-one miles north of Detroit—Krzyzewski's mind was on UNLV.

"Actually, I probably started thinking about them *before* the nets came down," Krzyzewski said. "It was good that we had five days to get ready, because we were going to need every minute to prepare for them."

The first decision Krzyzewski had to make was what do about the 1990 title game. His initial instinct was to pretend that game had never happened, that the last game of the 1990 season had been the semifinal win over Arkansas. He decided, however, to watch the tape alone. "In a sense, that was my punishment for that game," he said. "I figured, ultimately, it was my fault, so I should make myself sit through it."

The experience certainly wasn't enjoyable, but the more he watched, the more he realized that having his players watch the tape might be a good idea.

"To begin with, we were a better team by then than we had been a year earlier," he said. "We'd lost [Alaa] Abdelnaby, [Robert] Brickey, and [Phil] Henderson, but we'd added Grant Hill, who was a one-of-a-kind talent. Plus [Bobby] Hurley, Thomas [Hill], and [Billy] McCaffrey had all improved a lot as sophomores. And [Christian] Laettner had become a flat-out star."

There was more. Vegas had played a near-perfect game in 1990, and Duke had played an utterly imperfect game. "They were better than us," Krzyzewski said. "But they weren't *that* much better than us. I decided to show the guys why that was true."

And so, they watched the tape—painful as it was to relive for everyone but Hill, Antonio Lang, and Marty Clark, who hadn't been there that night in Denver.

"It made us understand that we could beat them," Laettner said. "I think Coach would have found a way of convincing us we could beat them regardless, but this put it right in front of us. It wasn't as if we thought beating them would be easy. I mean, they were 34–0 and it was no fluke. But we knew we had become a good team, a better team, since the Carolina game."

The media treated the week as if it was a coronation for Vegas. The Runnin' Rebels were attempting to become the first team since 1973 to win back-to-back titles, UCLA having won its seventh in a row that year. They were also trying to become the first team since Indiana in 1976 to go undefeated. No team since then had arrived at the Final Four unbeaten. In all, the Rebels had won 45 straight games dating back to their run to the national championship a year earlier. They returned four starters, including Anderson Hunt, who had been the tournament's Most Outstanding Player, and Larry Johnson, who would be the No. 1 pick in that June's NBA Draft.

Each of the other teams had good reason to be, as the cliché went, "happy to be there."

Kansas had won the national title in 1988 under Larry Brown but subsequently was hit by the NCAA with a one-year postseason ban and three years of probation for alleged recruiting violations. Meanwhile, Brown had left for the NBA and was replaced by Dean Smith assistant Roy Williams. That meant that Williams, a North Carolina graduate, was coaching Kansas, while Smith, a Kansas graduate, was coaching North Carolina.

Smith admitted it was a relief to return to the Final Four after an eight-year absence. "I think we all got a little spoiled when we had that streak where we went a lot," he said, referring to the period from 1967 through 1982, when his team reached the final weekend seven times in sixteen years. "It's nice to get back and appreciate how hard it is to get there."

Duke was in the Final Four for the fourth straight year but still hadn't won a national title. This, of course, led to all sorts of jokes from those not in love with the school about Krzyzewski's inability to win on the final Monday night of the season.

"Why does Coach K always leave the golf course after playing 14 holes?" went one joke. "Because he doesn't like the Final Four."

For the record, Krzyzewski never played golf.

He wasn't thinking about jokes, or even what his mother had said to him a year earlier after the debacle in Denver. He was thinking about one thing: 31–7. That would be his team's record if it were to beat UNLV.

"I started doing it during the first-round game of the tournament," he said. "Anytime any negative thoughts crept into my head, I'd just close my eyes and repeat to myself what our record was going to be when we won the game. Not *if* we won the game, but *when* we won the game."

That sort of mind game was going to be especially difficult on March 31 in the Indianapolis Hoosier Dome, beginning at about 9:00 p.m. eastern time.

....

Indianapolis was hosting the Final Four for the second time. The first time, in 1980, the games had been played in Market Square Arena, the 16,350-seat home of the Indiana Pacers.

The Hoosier Dome had been built to try to lure an NFL team to Indianapolis, and it had succeeded. With the promise that the new building would be open in time for the start of the 1984 season, the Baltimore Colts famously sneaked out of town on March 29, 1984, and set up shop in Indianapolis, opening the Hoosier Dome for football by playing an exhibition game there in August 1984.

Shortly thereafter, with the NCAA moving the Final Four into huge domed stadiums more and more, Indianapolis was awarded the 1991 Final Four. After that year, there would be only two more Final Fours played in basketball arenas: 1994 in the Charlotte Coliseum and 1996 in the New Jersey Meadowlands.

Duke had played the first two weekends of the tournament in domes, first in Minneapolis and then in Pontiac. North Carolina had played in the Carrier Dome in Syracuse. Vegas had played the West Regional in the

Kingdome in Seattle. Only Kansas hadn't played at least two games in a dome.

The shooting background in a dome is always different from the background in a regular arena because the building is so much bigger and the space around the court is so vast. Often it takes players a while to get accustomed to it. In addition, shooting the ball in an empty dome in practice is very different from shooting in a game with the building filled with spectators.

No one gave these logistics much thought going into Saturday's semifinals. This was UNLV's show, and the other three schools were just along for the ride.

"Being honest, we thought if we made the final, we'd be playing Vegas," North Carolina's Pete Chilcutt said years later. "We *wanted* to play Duke because of the rivalry and because we knew for sure we could beat them after the ACC Tournament. But we expected it to be Vegas."

The anticipation for the Vegas-Duke rematch was such that CBS selected it as the second game of the semifinal doubleheader. Normally, a teacher-pupil matchup such as Smith-Williams would have been irresistible for the network. But Vegas's rout of Duke a year earlier had been historic. More important, Vegas was unbeaten, and people had been talking all season about the Rebels being one of the greatest teams *ever*.

All of which meant that Duke was playing with house money.

"We knew how good they were," Laettner said. "But we also knew how good we were. Grant had given us an element we didn't have the year before. And Bobby was a different player than he had been as a freshman. We had more confidence in him because he had more confidence in himself."

Laettner and Hurley had a fascinating relationship. No one gave Hurley a hard time more often than Laettner. To be fair, Laettner gave everyone a hard time—so much so that his nickname among his teammates was "Asshole."

"He was an asshole," Hill said. "But he was *our* asshole."

But while Laettner never seemed to tire of giving Hurley a hard time, if someone from another team went anywhere near Hurley or tried to harass him, the first person to step in was Laettner.

"I knew, when I needed it, he had my back," Hurley said. "That didn't make it easier to take the stuff I took from him, but in those moments, it was comforting to know he was there."

Laettner and Hurley seemed to fit what had become a Duke stereotype: white kids who came from white-collar backgrounds.

Except neither of them did. Hurley's dad, Bob Hurley Sr., was a Hall of Fame high school basketball coach at St. Anthony's High School in Jersey City, New Jersey. Both his sons, Bobby and Danny, played for him there, and his teams won twenty-eight state championships even though St. Anthony's never had its own gym. Hurley's full-time job was as a probation officer, and Bobby was a New York City–style guard: hard-nosed, physical, and, though barely six feet tall, never one to back down from a confrontation.

Laettner looked more like a movie star than a basketball player. He grew up in Angola, New York, which is about thirty miles south of Buffalo on the New York State Thruway. His father, George, was a printer at the *Buffalo Evening News*, and his mother, Bonnie, was a teacher. Christian received a partial scholarship from the Nichols School in Buffalo, but it wasn't easy for his parents to pay his tuition. He worked part-time as a janitor at the school—no doubt one of history's tallest janitors at 6-11—to help cover the costs.

By his junior year, Laettner was being recruited by every major program in the country—including Duke and North Carolina. He was a good shooter for a big man and, in spite of his soft appearance, was never afraid to mix it up inside. As with a lot of Duke's stars, his decision to go to Duke had a lot to do with Krzyzewski.

"Don't get me wrong, I loved Dean Smith," Laettner said. "But the very first time I met Coach K, he acted more like he was already my coach than like he was recruiting me. No one else was like that. He made no promises about how much I'd play or how many shots I might get. He just said, 'You're going to come to Duke and become a great player. I believe in you.' He made me believe in myself.

"I knew how good they'd been," he said. "I wanted to go there and help make them better."

Duke had three genuine stars: Laettner, Hurley, and Grant Hill. The irony was that the one rich kid among the trio was Hill—who was Black. His father not only had been a star in the NFL but also had gone on to hold high-ranking positions with professional sports teams. His mother was a hugely successful businesswoman. The Hills lived in leafy Reston, Virginia, which was a long way from anything resembling an inner city.

"I think there was an assumption for a while that I'd follow my dad and go to Yale or go to an Ivy League school," Hill said. "But then, when I started to show some potential in basketball, I began to think I might be able to play in the NBA. So, the question became where could I go to school and get a degree that meant something and give myself the best chance to play in the NBA."

The three schools Hill was most interested in were all coached by future Hall of Famers: Dean Smith, John Thompson, and Krzyzewski. All were also considered outstanding schools academically.

"The good news for Janet and me was that we felt like we couldn't lose with any of the schools or coaches Grant was interested in," Calvin Hill said. "Fortunately, he was a good enough player that they were all interested in him."

Hill had some Magic Johnson in him. At 6-foot-8, he could play the point if need be, but he could also go to the basket and score inside. Smaller guys had trouble with him because of his size, and big guys struggled to deal with his quickness. Like Johnson, he wasn't a great shooter early in his college career, but he almost didn't need to be.

"People ask me a lot about the difference between our '86 team and the teams that won in '91 and '92," Amaker said. "I tell them the answer is Grant Hill. We had two great players with experience—Dawkins and Alarie. They had Laettner and Hurley. But they also had Grant. We didn't have anyone like that. Almost no one had anyone like that."

If Krzyzewski had one complaint about Hill, it was his gentle nature. There were times when, instead of making a play he could clearly make, he would defer to an older teammate. The only other contributing freshmen on the team were Antonio Lang and Marty Clark, and their playing time was limited, so Hill was always on the court with players who were older and more experienced than he was. Just not as talented.

"You could see from day one that he was special," Laettner said. "Every once in a while, he'd do something, and we'd all look at each other and say, 'Wow.' He had the wow right from the beginning."

. . . .

Duke was going to need all the "wow" it could get against UNLV.

"The best thing about Coach K showing us the tape was the message it sent," Laettner said. "He was telling us he thought we could beat them, that we shouldn't worry about what happened last year or be scared of them."

"Truth is, I thought about that game all summer," Hurley said. "I beat myself up over what had happened; it shook my confidence. But when I saw the tape, I realized that I was a lot better now than I had been then, and *we* were a lot better than we were then. I wanted to tip it off and play right then."

For players, the hardest thing about Final Four week is the waiting. They get into a rhythm during the season of having two or three days—maximum—off between games. If they play in the championship game of their conference tournament, they play for three straight days.

Which is just fine. Everyone is in shape, and both teams are playing on short rest. Players like to *play*, they like to compete. Once they know who they are going up against, they want to test themselves.

The drawn-out schedule of Final Four week is not helpful to this mindset. Through 1972, the semifinal games were played on Thursday and the championship game on Saturday afternoon. In 1973, the NCAA—encouraged by NBC—moved the semifinals to Saturday afternoon and the title game to Monday night.

The reason NBC wanted to play the championship game on Monday night—when it could garner more viewers—was UCLA. The Bruins, under John Wooden, had won six straight national championships beginning in 1967, when Lew Alcindor (later Kareem Abdul-Jabbar) led his team to the title. In 1973, UCLA's star was Bill Walton, who scored 44 points in the championship game on Monday night against Memphis State (making 21-of-22 shots) and led the Bruins to an 87–66 victory. In those days, the NCAA still insisted on a consolation game, and the third-place finisher was Indiana, led by a thirty-two-year-old coach named Bob Knight.

Nowadays, the semifinals don't start until after six o'clock eastern time on Saturday, meaning the second game doesn't begin until nine o'clock. And the TV executives insist on a 40-minute break between games, the better to sell more commercial time.

Final Four teams are now required to arrive in the host city by Wednesday night so they can be available for their press conferences on Thursday.

This is one of basketball's many "Bob Knight" rules. In 1987, his Indiana team didn't arrive in New Orleans until Friday afternoon. Because of weather delays, the Hoosiers arrived late for their open practice in the Superdome and, consequently, were late to their press conference. When the NCAA added a media day on Thursday, the teams were required to arrive the night before so they wouldn't disrupt the Thursday schedule.

Duke arrived in Indianapolis with little fanfare. The Blue Devils—along with North Carolina and Kansas—were seen as little more than fodder for UNLV.

What few people knew was that the Rebels were starting to feel the pressure of trying to go undefeated and win back-to-back titles. They had beaten 29 of 30 regular-season opponents by at least double digits, their 112–105 win at second-ranked Arkansas being their lone single-digit margin. On the road, against the team ranked just behind them, that hardly counted as a slipup.

But in the NCAA Tournament, they had only beaten Georgetown, a No. 8 seed, 62–54 in the second round and had a tough time with Seton Hall in the West Regional final before pulling away late to win 77–65.

One of the few members of the media who took note of Vegas showing a mortal side was CBS's Billy Packer. In his pregame "Packer Points," he noted that UNLV had not been involved in a true down-to-the-wire game all season, and if Duke could stay close, having been through numerous tight games, it might very well have an advantage.

Those words would turn out to be prescient.

....

The evening began with Kansas and North Carolina, a matchup that few had predicted at the start of the tournament. Dean Smith was in his thirtieth season coaching at North Carolina; Roy Williams was in his third coaching at Kansas. Williams had been a Smith assistant for twelve years and was the only member of the UNC staff who wept openly on the court in 1982 when Smith finally won a national championship. Unlike Smith, who never liked to let anyone see him sweat (or cry), Williams wore all his emotions on his sleeve.

Smith had been responsible for Williams getting the Kansas job in 1988, when Larry Brown had left soon after winning the national championship.

Williams had almost taken the George Mason University job earlier in the offseason but had been talked out of it by Smith. "You can get something better if you're patient," he counseled.

Two months later, when Brown became the coach of the San Antonio Spurs, Smith's advice turned out to be correct. Recommended by Smith (Kansas class of 1952), Williams was hired to lead the Kansas program. The Jayhawks had been ineligible for the 1989 tournament because of violations committed under Brown, but they had made the tournament in 1990 as a No. 2 seed before finishing with a 30–5 record after being upset in the second round by UCLA.

A year later, they were a No. 3 seed in the NCAA Tournament after a 22–7 regular-season record. But they got on a roll once the tournament began, upsetting No. 2 Indiana and No. 1 Arkansas to win the Southeast Regional. It was the third time in six years that Kansas had reached the Final Four but the first time with Roy Williams as coach.

Having been a No. 1 seed, UNC was the clear favorite going into the game, but the Tar Heels had a terrible shooting night. Three senior starters—Rick Fox, Pete Chilcutt, and King Rice—combined to shoot 8-for-36. Only Hubert Davis (5-of-8) shot the ball well among the starters. The key to the game, though, was Kansas freshman Richard Scott, who came off the bench to score 14 points and grab six rebounds. He was the one player off either bench who impacted the game, and that proved to be the difference.

The final score was 79–73, but unfortunately Kansas's upset was not the biggest story of the game. Dean Smith was—in the worst possible way.

Smith spent a good deal of the evening dueling with referee Pete Pavia. It was Pavia who had made the key block-charge call that went against Jay Bilas in the 1986 championship game. He was one of the most respected officials in the game, but he was fighting cancer and taking a good deal of medication to be able to work. Colleagues had noticed that there were times when he was short-tempered—not a great trait for a referee.

Earlier in the week, Pavia had worked the NIT championship game and ejected Oklahoma coach Billy Tubbs. He and Smith had never gotten along. Some officials were able to laugh off Smith's sarcasm. On this day, Pavia wasn't having it. He gave Smith a technical foul in the first half, which didn't seem important at the time.

But then, with Kansas in control of the game, Rick Fox fouled out trying to stop the clock. Smith had 30 seconds to send in a sub for Fox.

Instead of turning to guard Kenny Harris and telling him to go into the game, Smith walked him up to the scorer's table, arm around him as if giving instructions.

"He kept saying, 'Pete, Pete, how much time do I have,'" Pavia said later. "After the second time, I put up a hand and said, 'Dean, that's enough.' I knew what he was doing. Are you telling me Dean Smith didn't know how much time he had? Of course he knew. It was Dean being Dean. When he did it a third time, after I'd warned him to stop, I decided that was enough, and I teed him up."

Which meant that Smith was ejected. For a moment, no one realized what had happened. Then Smith, after another exchange with Pavia, walked the length of the Kansas bench, shaking hands with every coach, player, and manager. He may as well have shaken hands with the Jayhawk mascot.

It was as bizarre a scene as anyone could remember.

In the Duke locker room, Krzyzewski watched the scene unfold.

"I wasn't concerned about Dean getting tossed at that moment," he said. "That didn't matter to us. But Carolina losing *did* matter. I know I felt a sense of relief when I realized they were going to lose. It meant that if we won, we wouldn't have to play them on Monday night for a fourth time. It also meant that if we lost, we wouldn't have to watch them play for the national championship while we went home.

"It occurred to me that if I felt that, the players felt it, too. I walked into the locker room and said, 'Fellas, Carolina's just lost. I know how I feel about it, and I'm sure you feel the same way. Okay, Carolina's lost. Take a deep breath and feel a little bit of relief.

"'Now *flush* it. Your minds need to be 100 percent on Vegas.'"

The players listened. "Let's be honest," Hurley said. "We were happy Carolina lost, not because we didn't want to play them, but, well, we're Duke and they're Carolina. That was one of those little coaching things that people might not notice that Coach K did. It was smart."

The scene when the Kansas–North Carolina game ended was chaotic. Smith's top assistant, Bill Guthridge, was so angry that he tried to go after Pavia in the hallway under the stands. Fortunately, UNC sports information director Rick Brewer stepped in before things got really ugly.

As luck would have it, the chairman of the basketball committee was Big Ten commissioner Jim Delany, who had played for Smith at Carolina in the 1960s and was unabashedly pro-UNC and anti-Duke. (Why wouldn't he be?) He put out a statement saying that Smith had been ejected for leaving the coaches' box. Technically true, perhaps, but coaches were never teed up during a time-out for leaving the coaches' box *unless* they were arguing with an official.

"What's really unfair is that all of you are going to be talking about Coach Smith's ejection and not how well my team played," Roy Williams said after the game. "It shouldn't be that way, but I know it will be."

He was right. Kansas going from being a No. 3 seed to playing for the national title almost got lost in the shuffle after Smith's ejection. It was only the third time he'd been tossed in his thirty years as Carolina's coach.

. . . .

But the ejection and odd ending to the first semifinal game got shoved into the background by the Duke-UNLV game. If Krzyzewski had been worried about his team being distracted early, that fear went away quickly when Duke jumped out to a 15–6 lead. Vegas rallied, but the game seesawed throughout the first half, and the Blue Devils led 43–41 at the break.

"We walked into the locker room convinced Coach K was right—that we could beat these guys," Grant Hill said. "Their size was a problem, but we'd known it would be. We could guard them in their offense; the key was going to be keeping them off the offensive boards."

As it turned out, UNLV got 17 offensive rebounds in the game, compared to Duke's four, but the Rebels weren't able to pull away like they had all season against opponents that stuck with them for a half. Still, it looked bleak for Duke when a George Ackles follow-up basket gave UNLV a 76–71 lead. Glancing at the clock and seeing a little more than two minutes left, Krzyzewski decided to call a time-out.

"I thought we needed some kind of kick in the butt at that moment. It had been a very physical game. I felt like we were flagging a little. Then Bobby gave us the kick in the butt we needed."

As Krzyzewski was trying to get one of his players' attention to call time, Hurley was pushing the ball into the front court. To this day, Krzyzewski insists his point guard glanced at him but just kept going.

"I never saw him," Hurley said, laughing. "If I did, I was so intent on what I was doing, it never registered."

Hurley saw an opening in the Vegas defense near the three-point line, stepped into the open seam, and shot. The ball hit the bottom of the net with 2:14 to go to make the score 76–74.

Then Duke called a time-out.

"You could feel the momentum in the building change the minute Bobby hit that shot," Krzyzewski said later. "One second we were on our heels a little bit, and the next second we felt as if we had them on their heels. It was something you could actually feel in the air."

The game was now in the dangerous zone for UNLV that Packer had pointed out before tip-off. All of a sudden, the cockiness seemed to have been knocked out of the Rebels. Greg Anthony, their point guard, had fouled out on a charging call with 3:51 left and the Rebels up 74–71.

Many who were at the game now claim they knew Vegas became tight after Hurley's shot cut the margin to 76–74. Others insist that Anthony's absence in those final few minutes was the difference.

In reality, the difference was that Duke never blinked, even at those "pressure point" moments Packer had talked about that challenged both teams in a game that would become part of basketball history.

Rebel guard Anderson Hunt, who would finish with a game-high 29 points, missed a jumper, and Duke came down and set up its offense. Vegas was expecting the ball to go to Laettner, who already had scored 26 points.

But Brian Davis, who had come off the bench to give his team 21 minutes—the Vegas bench played a *total* of 23 minutes—and 12 points, flashed through the lane, caught a pass from Laettner, and scored as he was fouled, tying the game at 76 with 1:12 to play. When he made the free throw, Duke—shockingly—led 77–76.

Tarkanian called a time-out to set up the offense, and the ball went to Stacey Augmon. He missed, but Johnson grabbed UNLV's seventeenth (and final) offensive rebound of the game and was fouled as he went back up to shoot.

Johnson was clearly tight. Laettner had outplayed him the entire game. He had scored only 12 points up until that moment. An 82 percent free-throw shooter, he missed the first shot. Then, remarkably, he missed the second one as well.

Johnson had a strange free-throw motion, one in which he would seemingly release the ball only to hang on to it—almost like a Harlem Globetrotters trick move. Opponents knew about the false start and waited until he actually released the ball.

Except, in the frenzy of the moment, Duke guard Thomas Hill forgot for a split second and stepped into the lane too soon.

Given a third chance, Johnson finally converted, and the game was tied 77–77 with 50 seconds to play. That meant Duke couldn't hold the ball for a final shot. This time, Krzyzewski didn't call time, preferring to let his team run its offense without giving Tarkanian, a defensive wizard, a chance to set up his defense.

The ball swung to Thomas Hill, open near the top of the key, but his jumper was long. Laettner somehow got inside all of Vegas's big men to grab the rebound. Duke had four offensive rebounds the whole game, but that one was the most important. As he went back up to shoot, Evric Gray fouled him. There were 12.6 seconds left.

Tarkanian called a time-out to let Laettner think about the free throws.

"That was a waste of energy," Grant Hill said. "We all knew there was no way Christian was going to miss."

Al McGuire, sitting on press row watching, thought the exact same thing.

As did Krzyzewski. "I never brought up what to do if Christian missed a shot during that time-out," he said. "I just told them what I wanted to do on defense with a two-point lead. Most of which was to *not* let Anderson Hunt shoot a three."

Sure enough, Laettner's free throws touched nothing but the bottom of the net each time.

Hunt inbounded the ball to Johnson, the theory being let the best player create with your point guard out of the game. Johnson crossed midcourt and veered right, with Laettner giving him space. Johnson had attempted two three-point shots and missed them both, and Laettner knew he was much more dangerous going to the basket than he was pulling up to shoot.

"I honestly thought he would cut into the lane and drive, hoping I'd foul him since he was so much stronger than I was," Laettner said. "I was surprised when he picked the ball up."

Johnson picked up his dribble on the right wing, about twenty-two feet away from the basket. For a moment, it looked like he was going to shoot. But when he saw Laettner coming at him, he panicked and reversed the ball to Hunt, who had Hurley all over him.

With the clock about to hit zero, Hunt flung a long shot at the rim. It wasn't close. The long rebound went on a hop to Hurley, who, hearing the buzzer, flung the ball into the sky and began celebrating.

So did his teammates. Only one person didn't celebrate: Krzyzewski. He raced onto the court, palms down in the "cool it" signal.

"I was remembering what happened after we'd beaten Kansas in '86," he said. "We were so drained physically and emotionally that night that we weren't ourselves on Monday night. There was nothing I could do about how draining the game had been, but I could try to keep their emotions under control."

The players calmed down—a bit. "I saw Coach K with his palms down," Hurley said, laughing. "But after what we'd gone through to win that game, I was going to celebrate, at least for a few minutes."

He jumped on Grant Hill's back after releasing the ball. Hill had seen Krzyzewski, too. "I remember thinking, 'Oh my God, he's already coaching the next game,'" Hill said. "It was amazing."

Other than the quarter of the building where the UNLV fans sat in shock, there was chaos everywhere. John Wooden had been sitting with Quinn Buckner, the point guard on Indiana's 1976 team, the last to have gone undefeated. Wooden's UCLA teams had won seven straight national titles from 1967 to 1973. No one had won two in a row since then.

Wooden stood up, looked at Buckner, and said, "You know, Quinn, a lot of great teams have won one in a row."

He had heard all the hype during the week about Vegas being the greatest team of all time. He was happy knowing he wouldn't be hearing it anymore.

Laettner finished the game with 28 points. Davis came off the bench to add 15 points, while Hurley had 12—and seven assists—and Grant Hill added 11. Just as Amaker and Dawkins had almost saved Duke in the championship game five years earlier when the inside players had been exhausted, Hunt and Anthony almost saved Vegas—Hunt scoring 29 points and Anthony getting 19 before fouling out.

To this day, there are those who insist that Vegas would have won if Anthony hadn't fouled out. Maybe. But the same could be said if the block-charge in the '86 championship game had gone against Wagner and not against Bilas.

Wagner didn't foul out. Anthony did. Both results stand.

....

The problem for Krzyzewski after the victory was exactly what he had worried about when he rushed the court with his palms down: there was still another game to be played.

"I knew the Vegas win would be pretty hollow if we didn't beat Kansas," he said. "And I knew if we weren't able to bounce back physically and emotionally Monday night, we'd lose."

Fortunately, freshman Marty Clark, who didn't play a single minute in Indianapolis, and senior Greg Koubek, who scored a total of seven points, would play a critical role in Duke's preparation for practice and for the championship game.

As he got on the team bus to go to practice on Sunday afternoon, Krzyzewski noticed that Clark and Koubek were wearing brand new cowboy hats.

Without saying a word, Krzyzewski took Clark's and Koubek's hats off their heads. Then he signaled the bus driver to wait for a moment—the first time he'd done that since the Carolina debacle in Charlotte three weeks earlier—so he could lecture his team.

"Look, right now I really don't care that you guys beat Vegas," he said. "Neither does Kansas. That was yesterday. Trust me, if we aren't ready to play tomorrow, they'll beat us. And if that happens, you aren't going to want to deal with me.

"I don't like the way you're walking, the way you're talking, and I really don't like"—he paused to glare at Koubek and Clark—"the way you're dressing. By the time we get to the arena and get on the floor to practice, all of that better be behind you."

He sat down and suppressed a smile.

"I mean, really," he said later. "What was I going to get on them about? They'd beaten *Vegas*. That was an unbelievable accomplishment. But I couldn't let them think the job was done—because it wasn't."

Duke playing Kansas for the national championship was certainly fitting in light of recent history. The two schools had met in the national semifinals in 1986 and 1988, each winning once. The difference was that Kansas had been able to finish the job in 1988 by beating Oklahoma in the national championship game.

There was one other important difference: Larry Brown was coaching Kansas in those two semifinals. Roy Williams had taken Brown's place and inherited the NCAA sanctions that kept Kansas out of the tournament in 1989. It turned out that was the last year Kansas missed the NCAA Tournament. The Jayhawks made it fourteen straight years under Williams and have gone nineteen years (COVID-19 canceled the tournament in 2020) and counting under Bill Self.

Kansas had peaked at the right time, beating Indiana, Arkansas, and North Carolina to reach the title game. They had a superb backcourt in senior Terry Brown and sophomore Adonis Jordan, and in Mark Randall they had a fifth-year center who had become a force in his final season.

Duke had Laettner, who had become a genuine star, and four players who each averaged slightly more than 11 points per game: Hurley, the two (nonrelated) Hills, and Billy McCaffrey, who had started in the backcourt with Hurley until a midseason injury caused him to miss a dozen games. Thomas Hill had stepped into the starting lineup and played too well to be taken out. Additionally, McCaffrey had adapted without complaint to his new role coming off the bench.

When the championship game began, it was Koubek, the only senior starter (and the co–fashion plate), who got his team off to a fast start. He hit two corner jumpers—one a three-pointer—to give Duke a quick 5–1 lead.

It was also Koubek who started what turned out to be the most memorable play of the game by forcing a Kansas miss near the basket. Laettner rebounded and pitched the ball to Hurley, who, as usual, charged down the court. As he crossed midcourt, he spotted Grant Hill cutting from the right wing toward the basket.

"It was a turnover the minute I let go of the pass," Hurley said years later. "If I'd thrown a perfect pass, Grant would have had to make a great play to catch it. As it was, I overthrew it badly. It should have ended up in the third row. I was about to point at Grant and say 'my fault' when I saw him reach up to the ceiling."

Hill somehow timed his jump perfectly, reached high behind his head with his right hand, caught the ball, and, in one motion, brought it down and dunked it. To say it was a stunning play is a vast understatement.

On the CBS telecast, Billy Packer yelled in amazement. Jim Nantz, doing the play-by-play for the championship game for the first time, exclaimed, "Can you believe he got that high?" Packer followed with, "Jim, that ball was . . . going out of bounds! I don't know how he got up there to get it!"

The pass and catch are shown repeatedly every March during the tournament TV coverage. When Hill has been asked about it, he's laughed and said, "All I can see is my terrible freshman haircut."

When forced to go beyond the bad-haircut line, Hill said: "I saw the pass coming and realized my only chance was to try and grab it and dunk it. No way could I actually catch it. Instinct kind of took over."

"For the record," he added, "it *was* a bad haircut."

After making the play, Hill jogged back downcourt as if he'd made an open layup. He actually *pointed* at Hurley to give him credit for the assist.

"That was the funniest part of the whole thing," Hurley said. "The idea that I should get an assist for *that* pass."

Hill's dunk made the score 7–1. It turned out that Kansas never got even all night. The Jayhawks never quit, making runs to cut Duke's lead to three, but they were never closer than that. It was 42–34 at halftime, and in the second half, with Thomas Hill struggling to make shots, McCaffrey came in and went 6-for-8, including 2-of-3 three-pointers, to give the Blue Devils the extra boost they needed.

Laettner had played all 40 minutes and been banged around by UNLV's big bodies all evening in the semifinals, and he was still tired. Krzyzewski recognized this early and began taking Laettner out at any dead ball that was close to the sixteen-, twelve-, eight-, and four-minute TV timeouts. This gave him an extra minute or so to rest leading into the TV breaks. Laettner never found his shot from the field, but he consistently got himself to the foul line, where he made 12-of-12.

Hurley had also played 40 minutes against Vegas, but if he'd been asked to play 80 minutes in the title game, he'd have been able to do it. He was both relentless and tireless. He played 40 minutes again and finished with 12 points, nine assists (with a little help from Grant Hill), and three turnovers.

Duke led 70–59 with under two minutes to play, but Kansas made two quick three-pointers, the second off a backcourt steal, cutting the lead to 70–65. Out of time-outs, Kansas pressed again, and Duke had trouble getting the ball across midcourt. The Blue Devils called a time-out with two seconds left on the ten-second clock and 18 seconds left in the game.

All of a sudden, nerves were coming into play.

"Thank goodness I wasn't in the building," said then ACC commissioner Gene Corrigan, Duke class of 1952. Corrigan had decided early in the game that he simply couldn't watch from his seat. He left the Hoosier Dome and briefly went to a nearby bar, but, realizing almost everyone in the place was pulling for Kansas, he left and began walking around the massive stadium to kill time.

"Every time I looked at my watch," he said later, "it was about a minute later than it had been the last time I looked."

Corrigan was still circling the building as the Kansas band played its fight song, "Rock, Chalk, Jayhawk," for what felt like the one-thousandth time since the game had tipped-off.

Sitting on press row, I was at least as nervous as Corrigan. I flashed back to the Denny's, to the three championship games I'd seen Duke lose, and to the thought I'd had on occasion that maybe I simply wasn't destined to see Duke win a national championship.

Mike Lupica, who was my colleague at the time with the short-lived *National Sports Daily*, was sitting next to me. "All they have to do is get the ball inbounds one more time and it's over," he said. "Can they do that?"

"Shut up, Mike," I said.

"Whoo boy, rocky landing here," he said.

A few seconds later, the eagle landed.

With time short, Kansas was fronting the Duke players to try to steal the inbounds pass. Grant Hill was inbounding. As Hill was about to take the ball from the official, Brian Davis caught Hill's eye. He tilted his head in the direction of the backcourt; Hill caught the signal.

As soon as he was handed the ball, Hill acted for a second as if he was going to try to throw the ball to Davis, who had taken one step in his direction. Davis planted his foot and took off in the direction of the basket unguarded. Hill lobbed the ball to him, and Davis caught it and dunked it with 10 seconds left, making the score 72–65.

In those days, the clock didn't stop automatically in the final minute. Even if Kansas scored again, Duke didn't have to pick up the ball to pass it inbounds.

The game was over. The national championship had been won. Finally.

Outside the building, Corrigan saw people starting to come out. He grabbed someone by the shoulder and said, "Who won, who won the damn game?"

"Duke by seven," came the answer.

Corrigan took a deep breath, teared up for a moment, then raced back inside the building to congratulate Krzyzewski and his players on a game well played—though a game he hadn't seen.

Inside, the first player to get to Krzyzewski was the player who had scored the last basket: Brian Davis.

"We did it for you, baby," he said as he hugged his coach.

"I think we all felt that way," Laettner said. "We all knew all that he had accomplished, but that he hadn't won the national championship. We wanted to win it for him as much as we wanted to win it for us."

Krzyzewski hugged just about everyone in sight, tears in his eyes. When I walked onto the court and congratulated him, he ignored my proffered hand and pulled me into a hug (a tad embarrassing for a reporter) and said, "We've come a long way from the f—ing Denny's."

Indeed they had.

"People always said we weren't a good enough team in March," he said to Nantz and Packer a few minutes later. "We've always been a good team in March. We were just never quite good enough in April. Tonight, we proved we could be good enough in April."

The date was April 1. No fooling.

3

·············

BANNER TWO

It would take a while for Mike Krzyzewski and his wife, Mickie, to completely understand how life-changing it was to go from being a perennial contender to being a champion. In fact, when someone congratulated Mickie that night on her husband getting the national-title monkey off his back, she snapped, "There was never a monkey on his back."

She was right. It had been a gorilla.

Now, though, the gorilla was gone. Before 1991, Duke had been to eight Final Fours—three under Vic Bubas in the 1960s, one under Bill Foster, and four under Krzyzewski—without winning one. No school had come close to that many appearances without a championship banner; Houston was second with five winless appearances.

This may explain Krzyzewski's opening comment when his team walked into a packed Cameron Indoor Stadium the day after the championship game, almost everyone still bleary-eyed from celebrating.

Looking out at the overjoyed student body, Krzyzewski smiled and said, "Where should we put it?"

Everyone understood the reference. The building was already filled with banners from the previous eight Final Fours, the nine ACC Tournament titles, and the No. 1 national ranking in 1986. But none of those banners said "National Champions."

Now, one would have those two magic words.

No one knew at that moment how much the victory in Indianapolis would change the school's image. Duke had always been the "little team that *almost* could." The Bubas teams had never really come close to winning a title, twice losing in the semifinals and losing 98–83 to UCLA in 1964 in their only trip to the championship game. Foster's 1978 team had lost to Kentucky by a respectable 94–88 in the finals but never had a serious chance to win the game.

The only Duke team that had actually threatened to win the title had been Krzyzewski's 1986 team, which had come achingly close before losing 72–69 to Louisville.

And then the 1990 team got destroyed by UNLV.

Now, though, there were no ifs, ands, or buts: Duke was the national champion, and its four best players—Laettner, Hurley, and the Hills (Grant and Thomas)—would all be returning. So would Brian Davis, who had become the team's super-sub and defensive stopper. The only starter who had graduated was Greg Koubek. His minutes would be taken by sophomores Antonio Lang and Marty Clark. Backup big man Clay Buckley also graduated, but Krzyzewski had recruited two talented big men— Cherokee Parks and Erik Meek—to replace him. Parks was another of those highly sought-after recruits that Krzyzewski was now making a habit of landing.

The UNLV Runnin' Rebels had lost all of their stars from the 1990–91 team and had also landed on NCAA probation, the NCAA having postponed sanctions for a year largely because CBS had begged the organization not to deprive it of a defending national champion that had a chance to achieve history. Having declared the team ineligible to defend its title in 1991, the NCAA miraculously decided to rehear the case in October and ended up offering the school the chance to play in the tournament in 1991 in exchange for its ineligibility in 1992, when four of the starters from the 1990 championship team would be gone. Unsurprisingly, UNLV chose the 1992 alternative.

As it turned out, 1991 was UNLV's last moment of national glory. Tarkanian was forced to resign before the end of the 1992 season, and the school has been to a total of eight NCAA Tournaments in the thirty-two seasons since the loss to Duke, reaching the Sweet Sixteen once (2007) during those years.

. . . .

If the historic game in Indianapolis was the end for UNLV, it was a launching pad for Duke.

The Blue Devils began the 1991–92 season ranked No. 1 in the country, and they suddenly found their image on the national stage to be completely different than it had been prior to the upset of UNLV and the championship. No longer were they the school that had players the media found appealing because they were bright and funny and self-deprecating and won a lot of games, but couldn't win *the* game. Now they were the front-runners, and some people began to look for flaws.

Duke's image had started to change at the Final Four in 1986, specifically at the Sunday press conference prior to the championship game against Louisville. Louisville's five starters were a fairly typical group of college kids: most of their answers were marked by clichés, a lot of "you-knows," and references to "stepping up" and "giving 110 percent."

Then came the Blue Devil starters. They were clever and well-spoken. At one point, when the five players were asked if they would like to play in the NBA, Jay Bilas said, "I'd give my right arm to play in the NBA, but I don't think there's a lot of call for one-armed players in that league."

Most of the media was charmed. But not everyone, notably Mike Lupica, then of the New York *Daily News,* and Charlie Pierce, then of the *Boston Herald.* Both were nationally known and highly respected writers.

"What are these, the Cosby kids?" sniped Pierce, a reference to the

No. 1–rated TV show at the time starring Bill Cosby, Phylicia Rashad, and four good-looking, engaging, and funny kids.

Lupica, a close friend of then Kansas coach Larry Brown, was convinced Saturday's game had been stolen from the Jayhawks and kept insisting that Duke's players didn't even belong on the podium.

That day was the beginning of two labels that would be assigned to Duke Basketball by its detractors and follow it forever: Duke was "White America's Team" and the team that "got all the calls."

There were a couple of ironies in this. Louisville had four Black players on the podium that day; Duke had three. And if you ask Duke people and some unbiased others, Louisville won the national title the next night at least in part because of the controversial Pete Pavia call that went against Jay Bilas.

"The notion that we were White America's Team was just silly," Krzyzewski said. "We've had a lot of very good—great—white players, but we've had at least as many great Black players, dating to [Johnny] Dawkins and [Tommy] Amaker. Am I going to apologize because our players, Black and white, were smart and articulate and funny? No. If anyone has a problem with that, too bad. I'm proud of the way our players have handled themselves in dealing with the media and the public throughout the years."

There *was*, however, a racial element to the way people felt about Duke that went beyond the "White America's Team" label. It was one thing for opposing fans to deal with being beaten by teams led by great Black players. Basketball had become known as a sport dominated by Black stars, dating back to and including Bill Russell's Celtics teams; the 1966 all-Black starting five of the Texas Western team that stunned all-white Kentucky in the national championship game; Lew Alcindor's great UCLA teams; and, in the ACC, North Carolina State's 1974 national champions, led by David Thompson, and the North Carolina 1982 championship team starring James Worthy, Michael Jordan, and Sam Perkins.

There were, of course, exceptions: Bill Walton was a superstar at UCLA in the early 1970s, but he was looked at as a quirky, off-the-wall personality who happened to have freakish talent. Duke had, as Krzyzewski pointed out, excellent white players in the past. Jim Spanarkel and Mike Gminski had starred on the 1978 team, Mark Alarie had been the second-best player (behind Dawkins) on the 1986 team, and Danny Ferry had been the national player of the year in 1989.

Now Duke had won a national championship and was coming back looking for another one a year later. Some of the Blue Devil players undoubtedly were adored by much of the national media at least in part because they were white.

The "Duke gets all the calls" label also rankled Krzyzewski. "The reason it bothers me is because it takes credit away from our players and what they've accomplished," he said. "We didn't win because of the officials. Did we get calls go our way on occasion? Yes. Did we get calls go against us on occasion? You bet.

"I will say this: hearing that through the years helped me understand why Dean [Smith] got so upset when I made the 'double-standard' comment, and when other coaches in the league said Carolina got all the calls. They won because they were better than the rest of us, not because of the referees. The same has been true of us."

....

Laettner and Hurley both had personalities that were going to be either embraced or rejected by people who followed the game.

"It was almost like traveling with a rock band," said Mike Brey, who was an assistant coach on that team. "We were the champions, we had all our stars back, and people either loved Laettner and Hurley or they hated them. No one was neutral when we played."

This was especially true since the two stars played for a school that was in the same geographic location as its most intense rival, the school that also produced most of the media members who covered the two teams.

"I've always said that one of the things that makes us unique is that no matter how much we win, we will never be the most-loved team in the area in which we live and work," Krzyzewski said. "It's just a statistical fact that we're always going to be in the minority. We're surrounded by people who want to see us lose."

If anything, that fact is something Krzyzewski has used to inspire his teams. Just as Dean Smith loved nothing more than going into Cameron Indoor Stadium and silencing the Duke crowd, Krzyzewski loved going into the Dean Dome and quieting the Carolina fans. Smith's record in Cameron was 18–18. Krzyzewski's record in the Dean Dome was eerily similar at 17–19.

The ire that Carolina fans had for Krzyzewski and Duke increased tremendously after Duke began winning national championships. In 1997, Clemson coach Rick Barnes walked into the Dean Dome and introduced himself to John Dubis, the professional bodyguard who was assigned to escort the visiting coach to and from the court. Carolina had begun hiring professionals to accompany the coaches in 1993 after the two ushers escorting Florida State coach Pat Kennedy had trash-talked him while leaving the court after Carolina had rallied from a large deficit to beat the Seminoles.

Barnes and Smith had been feuding since Barnes's first season at Clemson in 1995, each accusing the other team of dirty play. The two men had nearly gotten into a fight at midcourt during a 1995 ACC Tournament game in Greensboro.

Barnes was not, by any stretch, popular in the state of North Carolina—even though he had grown up in Hickory.

"Are you nervous about escorting me on and off the court?" Barnes asked Dubis with a wide smile on his face.

"No coach, I'm fine," Dubis answered.

"Come on," Barnes said. "You can admit it. These people hate me, don't they?"

Dubis twice denied that anyone disliked Barnes, but when Barnes kept pressing, he finally said, "Yes coach, these people hate you."

Barnes nodded. "Do they hate me as much as they hate Mike Krzyzewski?

Now it was Dubis's turn to laugh. "Oh no, coach," he said. "They hate Mike Krzyzewski much more than they hate you."

That pretty much summed up the animosity between Duke and North Carolina.

Duke and Krzyzewski had finally reached level ground with UNC, beginning with the '91 championship. Smith and Krzyzewski each had one national title, and Smith had been to eight Final Fours. Krzyzewski had been to five, but he'd been to four in a row and finally broken through to win it all.

"It was definitely different in '92," Hurley said. "Because now we were the team with the target on our back—every time we played. What helped was that we were good enough to deal with it."

In fact, the Blue Devils won their first seventeen games, even against a difficult schedule. They rolled into Chapel Hill in late January ranked

No. 1, with five victories over ranked teams. Their only close game had come against Michigan in December, when they had to go into overtime to beat the so-called Fab Five 88–85.

It wasn't as if North Carolina had somehow gone away while the rock-band Blue Devils were rolling along. The Tar Heels were 16–3 and ranked No. 9 in the country. They still had excellent players like Hubert Davis, George Lynch, Eric Montross, and Derrick Phelps on the team.

The mood in the Dean Dome was electric, and the emotions of the Carolina fans were best summed up pregame by Jim Heavner, the longtime owner and operator of the Tar Heel Sports Network. "They're already making plans on how to keep the celebration on Franklin Street under control if Carolina wins," he said. "That's how big beating Duke has become."

Carolina got its win that night, 75–73, and students and fans celebrated up and down Franklin Street, Chapel Hill's main commercial strip. There were ten lead changes in the first half alone. Early in the second half, Hurley went down with what turned out to be a broken foot. He kept playing, although he was clearly hobbled.

"In those days, there were no X-ray machines in buildings like there are now," Hurley said. "Today, they'd have X-rayed me and taken me out. Back then, I just kept playing as best I could. It hurt, but we were undefeated, and I wanted to do what I could to keep us that way."

Duke came close, but they came up short when Laettner passed up what appeared to be an open three-point shot and drove to the basket, only to miss a short jumper before the buzzer.

The Carolina students stormed the court in the same manner that the Duke students had once stormed the Cameron court after wins over UNC. The celebration on Franklin Street went on deep into the night.

....

More important to the Blue Devils was the injury to Hurley's foot. When it was finally X-rayed, it showed a clean break. With the most difficult part of their schedule right in front of them, the Blue Devils were without their point guard.

Four of their next five games were on the road: at Louisiana State (LSU), led by Shaquille O'Neal; at Georgia Tech; at North Carolina State; a home game against Maryland; and at Wake Forest.

It was a tough situation, but Duke had a unique advantage: Grant Hill. The 6-foot-8 forward easily transitioned to point guard, while Antonio Lang took his spot up front.

Remarkably, Duke lost only once during that stretch. For a second straight year, Laettner completely outplayed O'Neal in Duke's victory over LSU. With Hill settling in at point guard, the team won easily at Georgia Tech and NC State. They then blew a big lead at home against Maryland, only to be saved by a follow shot by Lang in the final seconds.

The only loss, at Wake Forest, would prove to be one of the most important games of the season. Dave Odom had taken over as Wake's coach two years earlier and, even before recruiting Tim Duncan in 1993, had done an excellent job rebuilding what had been a fallen program. They made the NCAA Tournament in 1991 for the first time since 1984, and Odom would lead the Demon Deacons to seven straight NCAA appearances—1992 being the second year in the skein.

The Deacons were led by guard Randolph Childress and precocious 6-foot-7 forward Rodney Rogers. As had become normal, Duke walked into a cauldron of road noise, and the game went back and forth throughout a cold February Sunday afternoon. The Deacons led 70–68 with two seconds left, and Duke had to go the length of the court to get a shot—either a two-pointer to tie or a three-pointer to win.

"We had this play called 'home run,'" Laettner remembered. "We hadn't really practiced it very much, but it was pretty simple. Grant had the best throwing arm on the team, so he would inbound. I would come to somewhere near the top of the key, and he would throw me the ball. If the pass got there, I should have plenty of time to catch, turn, and shoot.

"The problem was, Grant threw an awful pass," Laettner explained.

"Wouldn't have been awful if his slow ass had gotten to the ball," Hill said, laughing.

In truth, it was Wake Forest's 6-foot-8 forward Trelonnie Owens who made the pass difficult for Hill. Odom put Owens on Hill to make sure he couldn't simply throw the pass directly to Laettner.

"I can still see him standing in front of me doing jumping-jacks," Hill said. "I was trying to get it past him on as straight a line as possible to Christian, but it went left on me. By the time the ball got near him, it was heading out-of-bounds."

Laettner made an attempt to get to the ball, but it did end up out-of-bounds. Wake inbounded, the Blue Devils had to foul, and the final score was 72–68. Duke's record dropped to 21–2.

"After we didn't run the play right that day, we practiced it a lot more," Laettner said.

It was a measure of what people in the basketball world thought of Duke that, even after the UNC loss and the Wake loss, the Blue Devils remained ranked No. 1 in both polls.

Hurley came back two games later in a 75–65 win at fourth-ranked UCLA. Hill returned to his small forward spot, but Lang, having proved his value in Hurley's absence, continued to get serious minutes off the bench. With freshman Cherokee Parks earning playing time as he improved, the Blue Devils were about as deep as any Krzyzewski-coached team had ever been.

On Senior Day, they easily avenged their loss to Carolina, beating the Tar Heels 89–77. The victory meant that Duke finished 14–2 in the ACC, winning the conference title by three games over second-place Florida State, which was 11–5.

After that victory, Laettner and Brian Davis spoke to the crowd about what was still to come.

Leaning on the scorer's table as if it was a couch, Laettner said, "Now look, we still have nine games to play. It's important that we know you guys are back here partying and having a good time after every game."

To play nine more games, Duke would have to make it to both the ACC Tournament championship game and the NCAA Tournament championship game.

No one on the team expected anything less.

. . . .

The ACC Tournament turned out to be a breeze. The Blue Devils cruised through games against Maryland and Georgia Tech and met North Carolina in the championship game for the fourth time in five years. The game was close for a half, as a Laettner three-pointer just prior to the buzzer gave Duke a 32–31 lead.

It was all downhill from there for Carolina. The final score was 94–74, almost identical to the 96–74 score the Tar Heels had won by a year earlier.

In the NCAA Tournament, Duke was sent to the East Regional as the No. 1 seed. The regional was *not* being played in the Meadowlands that year, having been moved to the Philadelphia Spectrum. Carolina went to the Southeast Regional as a No. 4 seed. Florida State, which was in its first year in the ACC, went to the West Regional as a No. 3 seed.

Both the Tar Heels and the Seminoles reached the Sweet Sixteen, but each lost to the higher-seeded team in that round—FSU to second-seeded Indiana and Carolina to top-seeded Ohio State.

That left Duke to represent the ACC in the Elite Eight. The Blue Devils had one brief scare in their first three games. It came against Iowa, the same team they had played—and beaten—in the second round a year earlier. Iowa liked to press for 94 feet and, during a brief stretch in the second half, with Duke leading comfortably, the press suddenly began to work.

The Blue Devils had handled the press so easily in the first half that they led 48–24 at the break. But they lost their focus midway through the second half, and suddenly the lead was down to eight. Krzyzewski called timeout, then let his players—notably Laettner and Hurley—yell and point fingers at one another for a moment.

Then he turned to them and said, "Okay, do you guys want to cut this s— and play, or do you want to go home?"

They decided to play and ended up winning the game 75–62.

On to Philadelphia they went, where a difficult game against Seton Hall was expected in the round of 16.

Krzyzewski and Seton Hall coach P. J. Carlesimo were friends, dating to Krzyzewski's days at Army and Carlesimo's days at Wagner. Like Krzyzewski at Duke, Carlesimo had endured a rocky start at Seton Hall, posting four straight losing seasons. With his job on the line, he had taken the Pirates to the NCAA Tournament in 1988 and, a year later, had reached the national championship game before losing to Michigan on a controversial foul call late in overtime.

Seton Hall had crushed Duke in the semifinals en route to that title game, and the program's turnaround had established Carlesimo as a star. In 1991, the Pirates had reached the Elite Eight and stayed close to UNLV until the game's last 10 minutes.

Now, they were back in the Sweet Sixteen as a No. 4 seed and had beaten LaSalle and Missouri. Duke people were nervous about the matchup, even though the teams were very different than the teams that had met three years earlier in Seattle. The only Duke player who had played a prominent role in that game was Laettner, who had been a freshman.

The Pirates came into the game 23–7. Duke was 30–2, having won nine straight games since the loss at Wake Forest. As they had done a year earlier against UNLV, the Pirates stayed close against the tournament's top-ranked team. It was 42–38 at halftime, and every time it looked like Duke might pull away, guard Terry Dehere (21 points) or forward Gordon Winchester (20 points) made a basket to slice the margin.

The Pirates also had a freshman backup point guard named Danny Hurley, who played 18 minutes but didn't score, missing all four of his field-goal attempts. His big brother, Bobby, also had a poor shooting night, making 2-of-7 shots. But he did contribute seven assists (to only one turnover), and the rest of the Blue Devils pieced together a balanced scoring night, with five players scoring between 13 and 16 points. Laettner had a rare off night from the field (6-of-13) but still scored 16, and Antonio Lang also had 16 points and seven rebounds.

Duke finally pulled away late to win 81–69. The sense was that with the Seton Hall win, the Blue Devils had beaten their toughest opponent on the road to the Final Four in Minneapolis. As it turned out, that sense could not have been more wrong.

. . . .

Rick Pitino had already coached one team to the Final Four—Providence in 1987, when he was the first big-time coach to embrace the new three-point shot. He'd jumped from there to the New York Knicks (he was a Long Island kid), but after two years there, he couldn't resist the idea of bringing Kentucky back to glory.

The Wildcats were fallen basketball royalty. They had won the national championship in 1978 (beating Duke in the finals) and had returned to the Final Four in 1984, only to be humiliated by Georgetown in the second half of the semifinal game. The Wildcats led 29–22 at halftime before being outscored 31–11 in the final 20 minutes and losing 53–40.

A year later, Coach Joe B. Hall retired at the age of fifty-six. He had won a national title, been to a second Final Four, and had an overall record of 297–100. Kentucky fans, who always consider winning not a privilege but a right, pushed him to the exit.

Eddie Sutton, a very accomplished coach whose 1978 Arkansas team had lost to Kentucky in the Final Four, was hired to replace Hall. The Wildcats won thirty-two games in Sutton's first season and reached the Elite Eight. But things began to unravel in 1988 when an Emery Express envelope sent from the Kentucky basketball office to Claud Mills, the father of highly touted recruit Chris Mills, accidentally opened in transit, and $1,000 in cash fell out.

The NCAA came to town, and Sutton was forced to resign after Kentucky went an unheard of 13–19 in the 1988–89 season. Kentucky was given three years of sanctions, meaning it couldn't play in the postseason in 1989 through 1991. Pitino took the job anyway.

The Wildcats went 14–14 in Pitino's first season in 1989–90, but his recruiting began to kick in the following season, most notably when he signed 6-8 Jamal Mashburn out of Cardinal Hayes High School in the Bronx. The Wildcats went 22–6 in Pitino's second season but still weren't eligible for postseason. A year later, they won the Southeastern Conference (SEC) title in both the regular season and the conference tournament and went into the NCAA's as a No. 2 seed in the East behind Duke.

Although Mashburn was clearly the team's star, averaging 21 points and almost eight rebounds a game, the media often focused on the four players who had stayed at Kentucky in the wake of the NCAA sanctions. None was a great player—the best was John Pelphrey, who averaged 12.3 points per game—but they became known as the "Unforgettables" because they had stayed through the bad times and been part of the team's turnaround.

When Pitino was asked why he thought those four players had stayed, he said, "Nobody else wanted them."

That was classic Pitino. The implication was that *he* had made them into good players. Pitino was (and is) a great coach. He also has one of the most remarkable egos in the history of sports. While he was coaching the Knicks, he cowrote a book modestly titled *Born to Coach*. He was the classic example of a coach who would tell people, "I coached good, but they played bad."

It turned out that the game against Duke in the East Regional finals was an example of Pitino's players playing *great* and him coaching not so great.

Kentucky liked to play up-tempo, and it got exactly the pace it wanted for the entire game. The game was frenetic right from the beginning. Mashburn, who would finish with 28 points and 10 rebounds, seemed to score whenever Kentucky most needed a basket. Laettner, who would finish with 31 points, did the same for Duke.

Duke led 50–45 at halftime, easily the closest first 20 minutes it had played since the Carolina game in the ACC Tournament. The Blue Devils stretched the lead to 12 early in the second half, and it appeared they would do to Kentucky what they had done to Seton Hall in the final 10 minutes.

But Kentucky's press was wearing on the Blue Devils—especially Hurley. He never came out of the game and finished with 12 points and 10 assists. But he also turned the ball over *eight* times, unheard of for him. As fast as he liked to play, he averaged a little more than three turnovers per game.

There was also a good deal of frustration on Duke's side. "It wasn't as if we didn't know what was at stake," Hill said. "We very much wanted to win two in a row, especially since no one had done it since UCLA in the seventies."

Pitino liked to sub 6-foot-9 freshman Aminu Timberlake in short spurts to give Mashburn help inside and to use his big body to wear down the other team's big men. Timberlake was no scorer—he averaged 1.1 points per game—but his presence in the game, although he played only five minutes, turned out to be important.

With just over nine minutes left, Laettner went to the basket and was fouled by Timberlake, who knocked Laettner off-balance and fell down in the process. Laettner needed two steps to regain his balance, and then, with Timberlake lying on his back on the floor, he put his right foot squarely onto Timberlake's chest.

Kentucky fans—and non-Duke fans everywhere—insist that it was a stomp and Laettner should have been ejected. Maybe if Timberlake had writhed on the floor as if in pain, the referees would have sent Laettner to the locker room. Instead, Timberlake jumped up, clearly unhurt, laughing and clapping in Laettner's face, as in: "I got you."

He *had* gotten him: Laettner was called for a technical foul, which was his fourth foul of the game. But Laettner had pulled his punch—or his stomp—just enough to not cause any harm and to keep himself in the game.

"He [Timberlake] had pushed me to the floor," Laettner remembered years later. "I made a note of it and made sure to be physical with him. Next thing I know, he went down right in front of me. It was a dumb thing to do, but the emotion of the game sometimes gets to you. I got a technical and that was it."

Of course, that wasn't it. More than thirty years later, there are many who still rail that Laettner got off too easy. In 2015, ESPN titled one of its vastly overrated *30-for-30* documentaries "I Hate Christian Laettner." After it aired, Laettner tweeted a video apologizing to Timberlake.

Ultimately, it was not mental errors, but turnovers—Duke would finish with 19 for the game—that helped the Wildcats rally, and the game went into overtime tied at 93 apiece. Three minutes into the overtime, Mashburn fouled out trying to block a Laettner shot. The teams went back and forth before a Laettner jumper put Duke on top 102–101 with less than a minute remaining.

Without Mashburn to go to inside, Kentucky had trouble finding a shot. Finally, Sean Woods, one of the "Unforgettables," drove the right side of the lane, pulled up from twelve feet, and somehow got his shot over Laettner's outstretched hand. It banked off the backboard and went in with 2.1 seconds left to give Kentucky the lead, 103–102.

Duke called a time-out. It looked as if the back-to-back championship dream wasn't going to happen.

For once, CBS didn't go to a commercial during a time-out. Instead, play-by-play man Verne Lundquist was composing on-air odes to Woods, Pitino, and Kentucky.

"Where did he find the courage to take that shot?" Lundquist asked color commentator Len Elmore.

"Well, the shot went in," Elmore answered, "but it was a terrible shot."

Elmore also noted that John Pelphrey had been calling for the ball under the basket, but Woods had decided to shoot over Laettner—who had come over to help when Hurley was screened—anyway.

It was Laettner who had the presence of mind to instantly call a time-out rather than react to Woods's made shot. When the Duke players got to the huddle, the first thing Krzyzewski said was, "We're going to win the damn game."

"When he first said it, I didn't really believe it," Hill said. "I figured we were going on spring break. But by the time we broke the huddle, I believed it."

"I think I was the only one who absolutely believed what Coach K said," Laettner said. "There's always one guy who's dumb enough to believe, right? In this case, it was me. But, looking back, there was reason to believe; I knew I could make the shot if Grant got me the ball."

The play Krzyzewski called was "home run," the end-of-game play that had failed at Wake Forest a month earlier.

"The thing was, because we hadn't pulled the play off at Wake, we worked on it in practice a lot," Laettner said. "If it had worked at Wake, we probably wouldn't have practiced it as much."

Krzyzewski remembered the huddle vividly. "I turned to Grant, and I said, 'Can you make the pass?' He said he knew that he could. Then I turned to Christian, and I said, 'Can you make the shot?' He just looked at me like I was a complete idiot for even asking."

There was one other significant difference between the Wake Forest game and the Kentucky game: the opposing coach. Pitino, the man who was "Born to Coach," at that moment made one of the all-time coaching blunders, choosing not to guard the inbounder.

Seventeen years later, Pitino said on the Dan Dakich radio show that he regretted not guarding Hill on the inbounds pass, but then he quickly insisted that his biggest mistake was telling John Pelphrey and Deron Feldhaus not to foul Laettner. That, according to Pitino, was the reason neither one was able to knock the ball down before it reached Laettner.

Wrong.

"I was surprised when no one came to guard me," Hill said. "I was wondering if they were going to call time-out to change the defense."

Kentucky actually had no time-outs left.

With no one guarding him, and with both Kentucky players playing behind Laettner rather than fronting him, Hill was able to step back and throw a strike to Laettner, who jumped up and caught it cleanly just inside the top of the key.

"Once I caught it, I knew I had plenty of time, there was no need to rush," he said. "2.1 seconds in that situation is an eternity. I knew I had plenty of time to get myself squared to shoot."

Laettner took one dribble to his left, then he turned to his right and released the shot. The buzzer went off with the ball in the air. It hit nothing but the bottom of the net.

Laettner spun and ran away from the basket in Hill's direction, arms in the air. Thomas Hill, who had been on the left wing, burst into tears, overcome by the emotion of the game and moment. Krzyzewski slammed the towel he'd been holding to the ground and went to give the shocked Pitino a hug. The rest of the Duke players piled on Laettner in celebration.

Laettner had pitched a perfect game: 10-of-10 from the field (one a three-pointer) and 10-of-10 from the line. Anything short of perfection on Laettner's part and Duke would have lost the game.

While Kentucky's players picked themselves off the ground in shock, Pitino headed for the locker room. Krzyzewski headed to the Kentucky radio broadcast crew, knowing that the legendary Cawood Ledford had just called his last game after thirty-nine years as Kentucky's play-by-play man.

Ledford was the rarest of SEC announcers in that he didn't scream every time his team scored and didn't complain every time a call went against them. Did he want to see Kentucky win? Absolutely. But he gave listeners a fair call regardless of the outcome.

Ledford's call of Laettner's basket was a perfect example. "Gooood!" he yelled. "And Duke wins it, 104–103. That's why they're number one."

Krzyzewski, a student of basketball, knew Ledford and knew that he had announced before the season that he was retiring. And so after shaking Pitino's hand, Krzyzewski headed across the court to Ledford and asked if he could come on the air for a moment.

Ralph Hacker, Ledford's longtime broadcast partner, remembered being stunned when he saw Krzyzewski approaching.

"I'd seen him go to Pitino right away," he said. "During the time-out, I'd said on the air that Kentucky was going to win the game. Cawood said to me, 'Not so fast. Remember, this is Duke.'

"Then, Laettner made the shot, and a moment later, Krzyzewski was standing in front of me. He pointed at his ears and at my headset, since it was too loud to hear. I gave it to him."

As soon as Krzyzewski had Ledford's attention, he put his hand on his shoulder and started talking.

"Cawood, I just want to congratulate you on a great career," he said. "You have stood for everything that's good about broadcasting and about college basketball. I know Kentucky fans are disappointed, but I hope they're proud of their team tonight. That was one of the greatest college basketball games ever played."

Hacker had first met Krzyzewski when Army played at Kentucky and Krzyzewski was a player. He'd gotten to know him while broadcasting NCAA games on radio for Host Communications, which had the radio rights to the tournament for years.

"I always liked and respected Mike," Hacker said. "But if I'd never met him before that night, I'd have loved him forever after what he did for Cawood. That was as close to speechless as I'd ever seen Cawood. To think to do it at that moment, after *that* game, was unbelievable."

The game is, in fact, considered to be one of the greatest college basketball games ever played. There have been documentaries done on it and books written about it. And it wasn't even a championship game; it was a regional final.

Laettner's "perfect" game against Kentucky was the zenith of the four regional finals he played in for Duke. The Blue Devils won all four games, and Laettner shot an incredible 31-of-34 from the field in them, averaging 24 points per game.

He also made two buzzer-beating shots, and in the 1991 Final Four he hit the two free throws that beat UNLV.

Al McGuire had never been more right in his life.

. . . .

The difficult thing in the aftermath of the historic win over Kentucky was that the season wasn't over. The Blue Devils returned home to find themselves being mobbed on campus, students still riding high about the breathtaking ending of the Kentucky game.

But the team had to turn around and fly to Minneapolis for the Final Four, which was being held that year in the Hubert H. Humphrey Metrodome. Cincinnati and the "Fab Five" Michigan team would meet in the first semifinal. Duke and Indiana would meet in the second game.

This was one of Bob Knight's best teams, certainly his best since the 1987 national championship team that had beaten Duke in the Sweet Sixteen en route to the title.

Point guard Chris Reynolds had also been recruited by Duke three years earlier before Hurley committed and Krzyzewski decided he was the point guard he wanted. Calbert Cheaney, a 6-7 junior forward, would be a national-player-of-the-year candidate as a senior; Damon Bailey, the heralded guard from southern Indiana who Knight had anointed as an eighth grader, was a sophomore; and 6-9 freshman Alan Henderson (who was from Indianapolis) had chosen Indiana over Duke, much to Krzyzewski's chagrin.

Indiana was 25–6 coming into the game and had lost the Big Ten title by one game to Ohio State. The Buckeyes had been given a No. 1 seed in the tournament; Indiana was seeded No. 2 in the West. Ohio State ended up losing in overtime in the regional final to Michigan, while Indiana crushed UCLA 104–79 in the western final. Indiana reminded many people of the 1981 team that had won three games to get to the Final Four by a total of 82 points. The 1992 Hoosiers won four games by a total of 87 points to reach Knight's fifth Final Four.

This, however, was a very different Duke-Indiana matchup than the last time the teams had met in the tournament in 1987. Then, Indiana had been ranked No. 1, and Knight was on his way to a third national title. Duke had surprised people by reaching the Sweet Sixteen, and almost no one thought the Blue Devils could win the game.

They didn't, but they hung close until the end before losing 88–82.

Now, Duke was not only the top-seeded team in the tournament; it was also going for a second straight national title. But that wasn't the whole story.

Earlier in March, *Sports Illustrated* had run a lengthy feature on Krzyzewski titled "Blue Angel." It was written by Alexander Wolff, long one of the magazine's top writers. The theme was simple: Krzyzewski had surpassed his mentor, Knight, to become the best coach in college basketball.

Krzyzewski talked to Wolff honestly about the fact that he sometimes got frustrated with constantly being connected to Knight. He was careful to say that Knight had greatly influenced his career, but that there were many others—starting with his parents and brother—who had been important in his life.

Krzyzewski wasn't trying to put Knight down in any way, but, naturally, Knight was insulted. He sent Krzyzewski an angry letter during Final Four week, telling him how ungrateful he believed he had been. The letter didn't really bother Krzyzewski; he understood Knight, and he also knew that the letter might be an attempt to distract him from preparing for the game.

Krzyzewski was fine when the game started. The problem for Duke was that Laettner was not. The guy who couldn't miss a shot in Philadelphia couldn't seem to make one in Minneapolis. He was 1-of-6 in the first 20 minutes and didn't get a rebound until midway through the first half.

"I think the numbers finally caught up to me," Laettner said years later. "You certainly can't expect to keep shooting the way I had in the Kentucky game, especially against a really good defensive team like Indiana. They doubled me a lot, and that certainly affected me. Everything that had seemed easy a week earlier suddenly seemed hard."

Laettner had made 20 straight free throws coming into the game. He missed his first two early. "Fortunately," he said, "Bobby was there to bail us out."

Hurley had 16 points in the first half, including four three-pointers. Every time it seemed Indiana was going to turn the game into a blowout, Hurley made a shot. Indiana led 39–27 with a little more than two minutes left in the half, but a Hurley three and a couple of Grant Hill buckets helped cut the margin to 42–37 at halftime.

"I think we felt pretty lucky to only be down five," Hurley said. "They clearly outplayed us. Maybe we were still a little bit drained from the Kentucky game emotionally. We were lucky that we got our act together before the end of the half."

"*Bobby* got our act together," Hill said. "The thing about him was that he was fearless. He knew with Christian struggling, someone had to step up and make some shots, and that's what he did."

Early in the second half, after Duke had cut the margin to 43–40, Knight got teed up by referee Ted Valentine. It wasn't one of his major tirades, but it was enough to draw the tech. Knight should have known better: Valentine, one of the best officials of his era, had a reputation for having a quick whistle when coaches got on him.

This time, with 18:06 left, Valentine nailed Knight while Duke was in the middle of a fast break. With Laettner struggling, Krzyzewski sent Hurley to the line. He made both free throws, and on the follow-up possession, Grant Hill made a driving layup to give Duke the lead, 44–43.

As it turned out, Hurley's three with Duke down 12 began a remarkable 31–6 run that stretched into the second half and ended with Duke leading 58–45 and 10:28 left in the game. Duke continued to hold a comfortable lead until the final minute, when Indiana guard Todd Leary, who averaged 3.6 points per game, came off the bench to make three three-point shots in less than a minute.

Hurley turned the ball over when he stepped on the inbounds line trying to inbound the ball. This gave Indiana a chance to tie the game, but Jamal Meeks missed a three from the corner, and the Blue Devils hung on. Antonio Lang made two free throws and Cherokee Parks one in the dying seconds of the game and Duke escaped 81–78.

Michigan, the darlings of the tournament, would be Duke's opponent in the final, having dispatched Cincinnati. Given that the Wolverines had taken Duke into overtime in December and the Blue Devils looked worn out, many people were picking Michigan to win the game.

Injuries were also a potential problem. Grant Hill had been playing on a bad ankle for almost a month. He had injured it during a practice prior to Duke's game against Virginia in late February.

"Christian and Chief [Cherokee Parks] got into it and were pushing and shoving one another," Hill said. "Chief went down and came down right on my ankle."

Hill had to sit out two games—against Virginia and at UCLA—but as luck would have it, Hurley was back in time for the Virginia game. He didn't play especially well, but against UCLA, he took over the game in the final minutes and led Duke to the win.

Krzyzewski had decided he liked having Antonio Lang in the starting lineup, so Hill had been coming off the bench since the injury—though he was still playing 30 minutes a game as the "sixth man." He'd retwisted the ankle in the Indiana game and was in serious pain in the locker room afterward. Worse, though, was Brian Davis, who had also hurt an ankle and hadn't been able to play in the last 10 minutes of the game. He was seriously questionable for Monday night.

And then there was the Krzyzewski-Knight soap opera, which, unfortunately, did not end with the final buzzer. As the players and coaches went through the handshake line, Knight made a point of not slowing down when he got to Krzyzewski. This is what is known as a "blow-by" handshake, which makes it clear that you really want nothing to do with the other person.

It was impossible not to notice.

Just to make sure there was no doubt, Knight hugged Colonel Tom Rogers, who was Duke's director of basketball operations. Rogers had been Knight's officer representative, the military liaison between the basketball team and the Army academic department. He had filled the same role for Krzyzewski when he coached at Army.

It was Rogers who had advised Krzyzewski not to follow Knight's advice in 1980 and take the Iowa State job that had been offered to him. Iowa State was a couple of weeks ahead of Duke in the interview process because it hadn't made the NCAA Tournament.

"Iowa State is a good job," Rogers told Krzyzewski. "But there are lots of Iowa State jobs out there. I think Duke is special. You should see it through to the end, one way or the other."

Krzyzewski turned down Iowa State. For years, it was reported that Knight had been responsible for Krzyzewski getting the Duke job. In fact, the key player in all of it was Rogers.

Rogers had retired from the army shortly before Krzyzewski moved to Duke, and Krzyzewski had hired him as director of basketball operations. In reality, Rogers was Krzyzewski's consigliere, the wise older head he turned to when he needed advice—whether it had to do with basketball or anything else.

I didn't think much about Knight's blow-by handshake when it happened. I'd seen Knight do it before; in fact, I'd seen him not shake hands at all with at least one coach—Illinois's Lou Henson—and I knew about the simmering tension between him and Krzyzewski.

I went to the Duke locker room to talk to the players and had left to head downstairs to press row to write my column (the locker rooms in the Metrodome were up a long flight of steps from the floor) when I ran into Mickie Krzyzewski.

Instantly, she grabbed my arm and said, "You have to go see Mike."

I was baffled; the game had been won, *and* I was on deadline.

"What?" I said. "Why?"

She simply shook her head and said, "Knight."

"You mean the blow-by?" I said. "I saw it."

She was shaking her head. "No, no, not that," she said. "Go talk to him."

No one knew—or knows—her husband better than Mickie Krzyzewski. I took her at her word, walked back into the locker room and to the back door, which I knew (from covering baseball in the building) led to the room where the coaches would be.

I knocked on the door. Tommy Amaker opened it a crack, the way bouncers had no doubt done during Prohibition. Fortunately, I didn't need a password.

When he saw it was me, Amaker opened the door, and I walked in.

The rest of the coaches were sitting in a circle: Krzyzewski, Pete Gaudet, Mike Brey, Colonel Rogers, and Jay Bilas.

The room was dead silent. For a split second, I wondered if I had been mistaken, and Indiana had won the game—maybe on a half-court buzzer-beater.

Amaker pulled up a chair for me and put it down next to Krzyzewski.

"What happened?" I asked.

"Nothing, I'm fine."

"If you're fine, why did Mickie send me back here?"

He looked at me for a second and said, "Because your guy Bob Knight is an asshole."

"Film at 11," I said. "I saw the blow-by. Did something else happen?"

Krzyzewski nodded and then told the story.

After the second Final Four game on Saturday night, the NCAA always sent the losing team into the interview room first because it was close to midnight by the time the game ended. This gave the winners extra time to meet TV and radio obligations on the court before their 10-minute cooling-off period began.

Ever precautious, the NCAA had curtained the hallway so that players and coaches could walk from the locker rooms to the interview room without anyone stopping them to talk or even shake their hand. There were no selfies in those days.

Duke had been headed into the interview room as Indiana was exiting. The two Hoosier players—Alan Henderson and Calbert Cheaney—stopped briefly to shake hands with Laettner and Hurley and then with Krzyzewski, who was trailing his players.

Knight also paused to shake hands with Laettner and Hurley and wished them luck in the championship game.

"I thought, 'Good, he's over what happened on the court, we're okay now,'" Krzyzewski said. "I walked up with my hand out and..."

Nothing. Knight acted as if he hadn't seen Krzyzewski and walked past him without so much as a nod. Krzyzewski was devastated. Mickie knew this instantly when she saw him coming off the podium.

Knight and Krzyzewski had always had a complicated relationship, dating to Krzyzewski's playing days at Army. Late in Krzyzewski's junior year, his father died suddenly of a heart attack. Knight left his assistant coaches in charge of the team and flew to Chicago to be with Krzyzewski, his mom, and his brother. Needless to say, Krzyzewski never forgot that.

Knight loved Krzyzewski's approach to basketball, but he always felt the need to make him—as with all his players—uncomfortable. During Krzyzewski's senior season, Mickie and a friend had come to a game at Princeton. Army lost by one point in overtime.

The next morning, knowing the team wasn't leaving to drive back to West Point until midmorning, Mickie drove to the team hotel for breakfast. Knight walked into the restaurant and saw his team captain having breakfast with his girlfriend a few hours after a one-point overtime loss.

"He went ballistic," Krzyzewski said years later. "He assumed Mickie had spent the night—which she hadn't. He walked up, screaming, said I was off the team and I'd better find a way to get back to West Point because I wasn't riding the team bus."

Krzyzewski bought a Greyhound bus ticket and got back to West Point. He went directly to the basketball office to see Knight.

"I was really angry," he remembered. "I told him it was unfair for him to think having breakfast with Mickie meant I wasn't upset about the loss. I told him no one had worked harder or cared more in four years about the basketball team than I had."

Knight would say later that he got exactly what he wanted: Krzyzewski wanting to *show* him how much he cared about the team. Army went to the NIT that season, and Krzyzewski shut down South Carolina star John Roche in the quarterfinals in a stunning Army upset.

When Krzyzewski got out of the army five years after graduating, his first job was working for Knight at Indiana as a graduate assistant. And it was Knight who recommended that Army hire him as its head coach at the age of twenty-nine.

But, as was often the case with Knight, the more successful Krzyzewski became, the more Knight was bothered by it. In 1986, when Krzyzewski first took a team to the Final Four, Knight walked around Dallas all weekend wearing a "Go Duke" button. Now Krzyzewski had won a national championship and had beaten Indiana in the Final Four. Somehow, Knight saw disloyalty in that.

"What did he expect me to do, *not* coach my team to try to win the game?" Krzyzewski wondered.

Regardless of how unreasonable Knight's position was, Krzyzewski was still hurt. That was why his wife had flagged me down in the hallway, and why his coaches were sitting around in silence after winning a Final Four game.

"F— him," I said. "He doesn't matter at this point. You're playing for the national championship on Monday night. *That's* what matters."

Krzyzewski looked at me. "I understand that," he said. "I'm fine."

. . . .

According to those who were with him later that night preparing for Michigan, he wasn't fine. He wasn't as focused as he usually was. Clearly, he was still upset about what had happened.

By the next day, though, he had found his second wind. Hearing the Fab Five predict during their press conference that they were going to win four straight national championships probably helped him get focused. Power forward Chris Webber, who would become famous a year later for calling the worst nonexistent time-out in history in the finals against North Carolina, said, "Our strength is that we don't respect anybody."

Duke's players were both amused and bemused by the Michigan players' comments.

"We knew they were good, and we certainly respected them," Grant Hill said. "But we were too close now to let someone beat us. We'd been seriously tested twice. We thought we were ready for just about anything."

Michigan was definitely the darling of the tournament at that point, and during the first half of the championship game, the Wolverines looked ready to give the Blue Devils perhaps their toughest test yet.

Once again, Laettner was struggling. He had finished the Indiana game with just eight points on 2-of-8 shooting and was having a similarly tough time against Michigan, specifically because of Chris Webber's quickness and the constant double-teaming he was facing. He actually turned the ball over seven times in the first 20 minutes while making 2-of-7 shots and grabbing only two rebounds.

Fortunately, the Hill "non-brothers," Grant and Thomas, took up much of the slack. Thomas Hill, often the unsung hero during the two championship runs, would finish the game with 16 points and seven rebounds. Grant Hill, back in the starting lineup because of the injury to Davis, was all over the court at both ends. He would finish with 18 points and 10 rebounds, and Krzyzewski would call his play the key to Duke's victory.

But it was Hurley who, even though he had a poor shooting night (3-of-12), once again played a major role, this time off the court. Michigan led 31–30 at halftime, and Krzyzewski remembered standing in the hallway listening to the Wolverines whoop and holler as they ran to their locker room, clearly convinced they were going to win the game.

Inside, the locker room was quiet for a moment, until Hurley lit into Laettner. "What the hell is wrong with you, Christian?" he yelled. "We *need* you to be you if we're going to win this f—ing game. Whatever the hell is going on, you need to stop it. You need to f—ing *play*."

Everyone remembered Hurley's tirade vividly—including Laettner.

"I needed a kick in the rear end," Laettner said. "I'll never forget Bobby standing over me and saying, 'We need you to win this fricking game.' [Hurley did not actually say "fricking."] We were always a team that got on one another when we needed it, especially Bobby and me."

Grant Hill laughed at that description. "Those two yelled at each other every day for two years," he said. "That night, we really needed it."

The voices in the room grew louder after Hurley's tirade. Whatever malaise had afflicted Laettner was gone when the second half began. Five minutes in, he cut behind a Grant Hill screen and hit a three—his first of the weekend—to give Duke a 36–35 lead. Michigan hung in for another few minutes, but with the Blue Devils up 48–45, Laettner drove at Webber and made a layup to make it 50–45.

It was over after that. Duke scored on twelve of its last thirteen possessions and outscored Michigan 41–20 in the second half, including 25–6 over the last seven minutes. The final score was an astonishing 71–51. Hurley, in spite of his poor shooting, was voted Most Outstanding Player.

Laettner shot 4-of-5 in the second half and had no turnovers. He finished with 19 points. His total of 407 points in twenty-three NCAA Tournament games are both records that will never be touched.

"Think about how good that team was," Hurley said. "I missed almost a month, Grant played hurt the last month of the season, and we ended up with two losses—both by two points—in thirty-six games. And we won the national championship. Pretty good."

To put it mildly. In the thirty-two years since Duke won back-to-back titles, only two other teams have matched the feat: Florida, which won the tournament in 2006 and again in 2007; and Connecticut, in 2023 and 2024.

Laettner and Davis went out with four Final Four appearances, two national titles, and the T-shirts that all the players wore after the 1992 championship game. They said, "You can talk the game, but can you *play* the game?"

A message for the Fab Five.

The second banner in Cameron Indoor Stadium was hung right next to the first one.

4

....

THE FIRST DROUGHT

Duke was now the undisputed king of college basketball. Krzyzewski had won two national titles—to Dean Smith's one—and made five straight appearances in the Final Four, six in seven seasons. Bob Knight still had three national championships, but Krzyzewski had beaten him head-to-head in a Final Four matchup and had been to one more Final Four than his mentor.

It was not, however, as if North Carolina had ever gone away. The Tar Heels were in the midst of a stretch in which they would reach at least the Sweet Sixteen thirteen years in a row. The last of those seasons, as it turned out, was 1993, when Carolina won Smith's second national championship.

The only key player to graduate from UNC's 1992 team was Hubert Davis. The loaded recruiting class that Smith had recruited two years earlier were all juniors now: Eric Montross, Derrick Phelps, Brian Reese, Kevin Salvadori, and Pat Sullivan. The heart and soul of the team was senior forward George Lynch, and sophomore Donald Williams had taken Davis's spot as the team's best outside shooter.

Duke had lost Christian Laettner and Brian Davis, losses that went well beyond their stats. Both were the unquestioned leaders of the team, along with Bobby Hurley, always willing to tell their teammates off when they needed it.

When I commented to Krzyzewski one night that Laettner might have been a pain in the ass but his personality drove the team, Krzyzewski smiled and said, "You never heard *me* say he was a pain in the ass."

Hurley and Grant Hill now had to be the vocal leaders. Hurley missed being pushed by Laettner, and Hill was, by nature, far more quiet.

"Someday Grant's going to figure out how good he is and take charge," Krzyzewski said during the season. "But it needs to happen sooner rather than later."

After going 10–6 in conference play, Duke lost in the first round of the ACC Tournament—for only the second time in ten years—to Georgia Tech, which went on to win the tournament. The Yellow Jackets, the No. 6 seed, beat top-seeded North Carolina (which was without Derrick Phelps) in the finals. Georgia Tech had to win to get into the tournament. Even after the loss, Carolina was still the No. 1 seed in the NCAA East Regional with a 28–4 record.

Duke was sent to the Horizon, a leaky, worn-out building a couple of miles from Chicago's O'Hare Airport, as a No. 3 seed in the Midwest. The Blue Devils cruised past Southern Illinois in the first round but lost to California two days later after Cherokee Parks, who had replaced Laettner as the starting center, went down with an ankle injury late in the first half.

It was a measure of how far Duke had come that their overall 24–8 record was considered a down season. In his final college game, Hurley tried to single-handedly save his team, playing all 40 minutes and finishing with 32 points and nine assists. For the first time in his career, Krzyzewski wept on the podium during the postgame interviews.

"I wasn't crying because we lost," Krzyzewski said later. "I was crying because I realized I was never going to coach Bobby again."

Carolina went on to beat the Fab Five in the championship game, helped immensely at the end by Chris Webber trying to call a time-out when the Wolverines had none left. As soon as Webber made the signal, all five Carolina players on the court began signaling "T" for technical foul because *they* knew Michigan was out of time-outs.

To this day, people talk about the Fab Five in glowing terms. Officially, they never even played in the NCAA Tournament because their 1992 and 1993 appearances were vacated for NCAA rules violations. And in those unofficial appearances, they never won the tournament.

....

Carolina was again back on top after winning the championship in 1993, and with everyone but Lynch returning and another touted freshman class—Rasheed Wallace, Jerry Stackhouse, and Jeff McKinnis—arriving, the 1993–94 Tar Heels were heavily favored to match Duke's back-to-back titles.

Only it didn't turn out that way. The Tar Heels bickered throughout most of the next season. Wallace and Stackhouse thought they should be starting, and from a pure talent standpoint, they should have been. But Dean Smith wasn't about to bench seniors who had been part of a national championship team in favor of freshmen, no matter how talented they were.

The Tar Heels were like the "little girl with the curl" all season—great when the players were focused on just playing, but not nearly as good as they could be when the locker room infighting reared its head. It can be argued that, even with a team that won the ACC Tournament and finished with a 28–7 record, Smith never had a more miserable season.

Carolina's two best games were against Duke—both double-digit wins, both examples of how good the Tar Heels could be. After UNC's 87–77 victory over Duke in Cameron, assistant coach Mike Brey laughed and said, "They hate us so much that when they play us, they forget how much they hate each other."

Going into the 1993–94 season, Duke had only one starter left from its first championship team: Grant Hill. He was now the point guard and clearly the leader of the team, having finally gotten Krzyzewski's message that he need not defer to anyone.

Cherokee Parks had blossomed into a fine center—not Laettner, by any means, but who was?—and Hill's fellow seniors, Antonio Lang and Marty Clark, were solid contributors. Duke also had a pair of young guards, sophomore Chris Collins and freshman Jeff Capel.

Thanks to Carolina's remarkable inconsistency, the Blue Devils won the ACC regular-season title before losing to Virginia in the ACC Tournament semifinals. At that point, Krzyzewski didn't know what to think of his team, which was 23–5.

Standing in a corner of his locker room after the Virginia game, Krzyzewski said, "You know, good for Virginia. They deserved to win. They played harder than we did. They wanted to win more than we did. If my guys don't figure out how hard you have to play to win in March, we won't be around for very long when the tournament starts."

Somehow, they figured it out. They were given a No. 2 seed in the Southeast Regional and won twice in St. Petersburg, Florida, beating Texas Southern and Michigan State.

By sheer coincidence (ha!), Kentucky was the No. 3 seed in that region. The NCAA was hoping for a rematch of the "Laettner game." Kentucky played the first game of the Sunday afternoon second-round doubleheader in the miserable building known back then as the Suncoast Dome. It is now called Tropicana Field and is every bit as miserable today—regardless of the sport—as it was then. The late Sparky Anderson, the Hall of Fame manager of the Cincinnati Reds and Detroit Tigers, once said of the building: "It's the only place I've ever been where it's always overcast—indoors."

On that sunny afternoon (outdoors) in March, Kentucky let down both the NCAA Tournament committee and CBS by losing to sixth-seeded Marquette 75–63. There was never a more blatant example of coaching hubris than this game.

Rick Pitino loved to pressure teams for 94 feet, turn them over, and blow them out of the building. But Marquette had a point guard named Tony Smith, who couldn't shoot a lick but was a jet in the open court. He consistently beat the Kentucky pressure, found open teammates, and the

Warriors (now Golden Eagles) built a big lead and made their free throws when Kentucky tried to rally.

After the game, Pitino sat on the podium with his three brokenhearted seniors and said, "This was a Kentucky team that lacked leadership, lacked chemistry, and lacked toughness."

The Wildcats had finished 28–7.

Much to the chagrin of CBS, Duke played Marquette in the round of 16. Making no attempt to press, the Blue Devils held Marquette to 17-of-54 shooting from the field and won 59–49. That put them in the regional final against top-seeded Purdue, which was led by national player of the year Glenn Robinson.

Purdue had been something of a postseason bugaboo opponent for Duke. In 1980, after Bill Foster's last team had stunned Kentucky in the round of 16 on Kentucky's home court, the Blue Devils had lost the regional final to Purdue. A year later, with both teams under new coaches—Mike Krzyzewski at Duke and Gene Keady at Purdue—the Boilermakers beat the Blue Devils in an NIT quarterfinal game played at Purdue.

Now Keady was still seeking his first trip to the Final Four; Krzyzewski was trying to get to his seventh in nine seasons. Once again, Duke's defense proved to be the game's key ingredient.

Purdue was led by the 6-foot-8 Robinson, who had beaten out Hill for player of the year across the board nationally. There was good reason for this: Robinson had averaged 30.3 points and 12.3 rebounds per game. But there was one thing Hill could do better than Robinson: play defense. And he brought his teammates with him.

Robinson had his worst game of the season, shooting 6-of-22 and finishing with 13 points. Duke led most of the game, and Capel and Lang, with 19 points apiece, put the game away with big baskets late.

The final score was 69–60 Duke. The win put Krzyzewski's team into the Final Four for the seventh time in nine years. Only John Wooden, who had taken UCLA to the last weekend eleven times in twelve years, could top those numbers.

The Final Four was in the Charlotte Coliseum—the second-to-last time it would be played in a true basketball arena.

Duke beat Florida and Arkansas beat Arizona in the semifinal games, creating a rematch of the 1990 semifinals to decide the championship.

Monday night's game brought President Bill Clinton, a longtime Arkansas fan, to the arena, creating chaos and delays for fans trying to get into parking lots and through security to get into the game.

It was worth the effort. The game went back-and-forth the entire night. Grant Hill, playing his final college game, tied the score at 70 with a little more than a minute remaining. The Razorback who had hurt Duke the most during the game was center Corliss Williamson. Parks had done his best to keep Williamson out of the post, but he was playing on a strained left knee, which he hurt late in the Florida game.

Williamson had 24 points, and when the ball went to him in the post, Lang instinctively left his man, Scotty Thurman, to help, even though Krzyzewski had told him not to leave Thurman, who was just 5-of-12 from the field at that moment but still Arkansas's best outside shooter.

Seeing Lang moving in his direction, Williamson alertly pitched the ball to Thurman, who was in his shooting motion as he caught the ball. Lang scrambled to get back to him, but Thurman's three-pointer cleared Lang's fingertips and hit the bottom of the net with 50 seconds to play. That proved to be the difference. Chris Collins had a three of his own go all the way down before rimming out seconds later, and Arkansas held on for a 76–72 victory.

. . . .

Duke had come within inches of winning three national titles in four years— a dream come true for what had once been the team that "couldn't quite get there" each spring. There was no way to know that this dream would become a nightmare for most of the next five years.

It had actually started during that 1993–94 season. Both Krzyzewskis, Mike and Mickie, had begun to have wanderlust. The NBA's Boston Celtics had wooed Krzyzewski for a time back in 1990, and the NBA was still interested in him. With two national championship banners hanging in Cameron, Krzyzewski was more inclined to listen this time around.

Both Mike and Mickie—especially Mickie—felt that he was underappreciated by Duke. Although Mike was making a lot more money than the $40,000 a year he had been paid when he first arrived, both believed he was underpaid. What's more, Tom Butters had semiretired and was spending most of the winter at his home in Florida, playing golf every day.

On the night Duke lost to Arkansas, Mickie Krzyzewski stood outside the Duke locker room with her three daughters and sighed. "It would have been nice for dad to win one more national championship and then leave," she said.

Jamie, the youngest daughter, who was twelve, glared at her mother for a moment and then said, "Don't talk that way. We're not leaving."

She then stalked away, saying, "I don't want to listen to this anymore."

But Mike and Mickie were listening. Both the Miami Heat and the Portland Trail Blazers were looking for a coach and were willing to pay a lot of money for the right one. NBA commissioner David Stern called Krzyzewski repeatedly to tell him he would do anything necessary to help him decide the NBA was the right place for him.

Keith Drum, Krzyzewski's only early media supporter in North Carolina, was working for the Portland Trail Blazers by then. At the request of Portland general manager Brad Greenberg, he called Krzyzewski to gauge his interest.

"I didn't feel as if he was all that interested," Drum said. "He did ask at one point how much the job would pay—it was considerably more than Duke—but I still didn't think he was interested."

Mike and Mickie decided to go away together to a resort in Florida to clear their minds and add up the pros and cons of staying at Duke or leaving for the NBA. When they came home, they had made up their minds: Mike would stay.

In the end, Krzyzewski had decided that coaching at the college level was more gratifying than coaching in the NBA. He had more influence on the lives of his players, and he didn't have to coach 100-plus games a year to win a championship. He was only forty-seven, and if he felt like trying the NBA at a later time, opportunities would no doubt be there.

That decided, Krzyzewski began to prepare for the 1994–95 season. Marty Clark, Antonio Lang, and, most important, Grant Hill would be gone. Cherokee Parks would be back for his senior season, and his 6-foot-10 classmate Eric Meek had become a solid player inside. Chris Collins and Jeff Capel would be joined in the backcourt by three talented freshmen: Steve Wojciechowski, Trajan Langdon, and Ricky Price.

A solid team, no doubt, but there was no one like Laettner, Hurley, or Hill. And no one who could play defense the way Brian Davis and Thomas Hill had on the championship teams.

"I thought we had the potential to be good," Krzyzewski said. "Not great, but good or maybe very good."

To be very good, Duke would need Krzyzewski at his very best. Mentally, he was ready for the challenge. The problem was, his body wasn't cooperating. His back began to give him trouble during the summer, and doctors advised him to have surgery and get it over with even though he would be unable to coach for at least a month. Do it now, they said, and you won't miss any games.

But Krzyzewski didn't want to miss *anything*.

"He was doing his old army 'mind-over-matter' trick," Mickie remembered. "If you tell yourself you can do something, even if you're in pain, you can do it."

By the time practice started in October, it was apparent the trick wasn't working. Krzyzewski couldn't stand up for very long during practice. The pain wasn't getting any better but getting worse. It was apparent he wasn't going to make it through the season without something being done.

He finally opted for surgery in late October. The doctors told him he needed to stay away from practice or anything that would stress his back for four to six weeks.

He was back at practice in two weeks.

"The mind-over-matter thing again," Mickie said.

The season started benignly enough. There were losses to Connecticut and Iowa (each getting some small measure of revenge for NCAA Tournament losses) and wins over Michigan and Georgia Tech—the second win coming in Hawaii because, for some reason, two ACC teams had been invited to Honolulu's Rainbow Classic.

The win over the Yellow Jackets left Duke with an 8–2 record. On the plane flight home, Krzyzewski had to stand the whole way because he was in so much pain. The Blue Devils won their final nonconference game against South Carolina State and then opened ACC play with a shocking 75–70 loss at home to Clemson, dropping their record to 9–3.

Two days later, the team was scheduled to fly to Georgia Tech. That was the morning when Mickie Krzyzewski informed her husband that he had a two o'clock doctor's appointment, and if he didn't show up, she was leaving him.

"Someone had to make it stop," Mickie said years later. "I realized I was the only person who *might* be able to do it."

"We're flying to Atlanta at one o'clock," Mike said.

"I'll be at the doctor's office at two," Mickie answered. "I hope you'll be there."

To this day, Mickie Krzyzewski doesn't honestly know what she would have done if Mike had called her bluff. But he showed up at the doctor's office and left Pete Gaudet in charge of the team.

As it turned out, he didn't coach again that season. The doctors told him he couldn't coach again because he wasn't healed physically, and he was so emotionally stressed that he wasn't allowing himself to get better.

When Duke announced that Krzyzewski was taking a leave of absence, the Carolina-rabid members of the North Carolina media had a field day. Krzyzewski's back, they insisted, had really started to hurt when he got a good look at his team—ha-ha-ha-ha. The evil "rat-faced-one," as the *Daily Tar Heel* had called him in the past, was finally being brought down.

There was no doubt that Krzyzewski—and his team—had been brought down. But the woes of the team on the court were, for a long time, the least of his problems. For a while, he was convinced he had cancer and was going to die just as Jim Valvano had done almost two years earlier.

"I was forty-seven, the same age Jimmy was when he died," he said. "The problem was in my back, the same as Jimmy. I was a basketball coach with three daughters being treated at Duke hospital, just like Jimmy. I was convinced I had the same thing Jimmy had, and I was going to die just like Jimmy had died."

Krzyzewski didn't have cancer. He had a back and a brain that both needed rest. Once again, his military training affected his decision making. He had been taught at West Point that, dating to the ancient Greeks, when a general's army had been defeated, the honorable thing was for him to fall on his sword. Krzyzewski believed that he had let his troops down because he could no longer lead them and that he should metaphorically fall on his sword by resigning.

He went to Tom Butters's house one night late in January, planning to resign. Butters knew Krzyzewski's plan before he arrived.

"I knew Mike, I knew he would feel he had failed his players, he had failed Duke, and he had failed me," he said. "There was no way I was going to let him resign."

When Krzyzewski told him he believed resigning was the right thing to do, Butters looked at him and said, "You're not resigning, and I'm going to tell you why: there is no one else I want to coach this team next year. You are going to bring us back."

Once Krzyzewski understood that he wasn't going to coach again that season but *was* going to coach again the next season, he began to get better. His team, however, was a mess.

Under Gaudet, the Blue Devils went 4–15, losing one close game after another. They lost in double overtime to Virginia, in double overtime to North Carolina (after blowing a late 13-point lead), twice to Maryland by two points, and by one to Wake Forest. The case can certainly be made that Krzyzewski's presence in any or all of those games might well have been the difference.

"I never wanted to lose to Duke, but beating them without Mike was like not really beating them," Dean Smith said. "I wanted them at their best. They couldn't possibly be their best without Mike."

It wasn't as simple as Gaudet not being as good a coach as Krzyzewski; it was that the entire staff was turned upside down as everyone was forced to play a different role.

"Pete's *voice* was different than Mike's," Mike Brey said. "He was more analytical, more of a soother than Mike. I remember one night we were getting our butts beat at halftime, and Pete was calmly trying to make adjustments. I finally lost it. I said, 'F— it, Pete, enough with this. It's time we got out there and play like f—ing men!'"

Brey smiled. "So we went out and got our butts beat again in the second half. Lot of good I did."

The season became a walk on coals for everyone. Duke finished dead last in the ACC but managed to beat NC State in the eight-nine play-in game of the ACC Tournament before getting manhandled by Wake Forest in what had euphemistically become known as the "quarterfinals" after the eight-nine game was added in 1992.

The loss to Wake was a relief for everyone. The coaches had been horrified when Dick Vitale had suggested during a game that Duke be invited to the NIT, regardless of their record, because it was Duke. "I remember thinking, 'Dick, please, please shut up,'" Tommy Amaker said. "We all just wanted it over."

There was one more headache to deal with before Duke could move on to turning things around. Under NCAA rules, Duke's last nineteen games were counted as part of Gaudet's coaching record. Had Krzyzewski returned to the bench before the end of the season, the games Gaudet coached would have counted as part of Krzyzewski's record. But Krzyzewski had not returned, so the wins and losses were Gaudet's. If the team had been 15–4 instead of 4–15, that record would have belonged to Gaudet.

But the Duke-phobes didn't want that to be the story. Two writers in particular spread the word that Duke and Krzyzewski had pleaded with the NCAA to make the 4–15 part of Gaudet's record. To *this day*, there are those who will insist that's the case. The truth was—and is—irrelevant to them.

. . . .

The next three seasons saw steady improvement. Krzyzewski made one huge change to his coaching staff when he returned, letting his longtime friend Gaudet go. Brey was also gone, having taken the head coaching job at Delaware. Bilas had finished law school and was practicing law and beginning what would become an epic broadcasting career.

The most experienced of the assistant coaches was now Amaker, who had given up graduate school to become a full-time assistant and was now thirty. Quin Snyder had finished two graduate degrees and joined the staff at the age of twenty-eight. Tim O'Toole would be the last non–Duke graduate to work for Krzyzewski. He was thirty-one and had worked for Jim Boeheim the previous three seasons. O'Toole was as animated as Amaker and Snyder were studious. He never walked into a room; he *burst* into a room.

"I needed my staff to be younger and more aggressive at that point in my career," Krzyzewski said later. "For years, I was the young, aggressive coach, and Pete was the wise old head who helped calm me down. When I came back after '95, I realized I had become the wise old head. What I needed, especially in recruiting, were guys who were young and aggressive."

The 1995–96 season wasn't an easy one by any means. Duke started 0–4 in ACC play, and there were those—including Krzyzewski—who wondered if the glory days were over.

The season-turning, and maybe program-changing, game came at North Carolina State. The Wolfpack were playing desperate basketball, trying to save coach Les Robinson's job. They had an outstanding center in Todd Fuller—who would be the 11th pick in that summer's NBA Draft—and a group of solid role players. They were 11–4 coming into the game, with two losses in Hawaii to ranked teams (No. 1 Massachusetts and No. 12 Illinois) and conference losses on the road to North Carolina and Virginia. They had beaten Florida State at home and badly needed to hold serve in Reynolds Coliseum against a Duke team that was clearly struggling.

The Wolfpack led most of the night, but Duke wouldn't go away. The Blue Devils finally closed the gap to 70–68. With the clock ticking towards zero, Chris Collins came open just outside the three-point line and fired a shot. It hit the front rim, crawled over it, and fell through the basket. Duke won 71–70.

Krzyzewski was so drained by the win, and by the twelve months that had come before, that he cried on the shoulder of his oldest daughter, Debbie, outside the locker room. Mickie had stopped going to road games because of the behavior of opposing fans, so it was Debbie's shoulder that Krzyzewski had to cry on.

"It's impossible to say how important that win was, and how important Chris's shot was, for us," Krzyzewski said. "He was our senior leader that season, and he's never gotten the credit for what he accomplished that season. Everything that came after that started with that game, that season, and what Chris did."

Duke went 8–4 the rest of the ACC regular season, but Collins broke his foot in the season finale against North Carolina and had to sit out an ACC Tournament loss to Maryland.

The Blue Devils were sent to the Southeast Regional as a No. 8 seed in the NCAAs but were beaten handily by No. 9 seed Eastern Michigan 75–60. The Eagles were led by Earl Boykins, a 5-foot-5 whirling dervish who scored 23 points and then went on to play twelve years in the NBA, even though he was not drafted.

Three days later, North Carolina was similarly blown out in the second round by Texas Tech. This meant that for the first time since 1979, neither Duke nor North Carolina played in the tournament's second weekend. Texas Tech would later become one of two teams in the East Regional to have their tournament games vacated because of NCAA violations. The other one was top-seeded Massachusetts, which reached the Final Four and lost to Kentucky in the semifinals, only to have its postseason erased from the record books.

Duke added one important freshman the following season: 6-foot-6 swingman Chris Carrawell, whose defensive skills reminded people a little bit of Billy King's because he could guard players from point guard to center. But the Blue Devils also returned sophomore shooting guard Trajan Langdon, who had to sit out the '96 season with a knee injury.

The season began rockily with an 85–69 loss in the preseason NIT final to Indiana in Madison Square Garden. Krzyzewski and Knight still hadn't spoken since the Minneapolis Final Four, and Krzyzewski decided before the game that it was time for him to offer an olive branch.

As the teams finished warming up, Krzyzewski walked down to the Indiana bench and shook hands with the Indiana assistants, then stood and waited for Knight to come out of the locker room. Knight always liked to make his pregame entrance late, usually waiting until the clock was under a minute before he walked to the bench.

Sure enough, Knight came walking out with famed horse trainer D. Wayne Lucas by his side. Knight could never stand to be alone, especially just before a game, and he often had outsiders sit with him (for one season it was me) while he waited to come out. Knight looked right at Krzyzewski from a few feet away, then turned his back on him to tell Lucas some story that absolutely had to be told at that moment. The clock ran to zero, the buzzer sounded, and Knight was still talking. Krzyzewski shrugged and walked back to his own bench.

After that game, Krzyzewski sat with his coaches and me, shook his head, and said, "That's it. That's the period on the end of the sentence. I'm done."

The period turned out to be just a semicolon, although it didn't change into one for another five years.

Duke followed the Indiana loss with a home-court loss to Michigan (the Fab Five were long gone) but bounced back to beat fourth-ranked Villanova in Philadelphia. The Blue Devils began the ACC season at 3–3, including a last-second loss at Maryland to the seventh-ranked Terrapins.

That was when Krzyzewski threw a temper tantrum. During his Monday meeting with the assistant coaches the day after the Maryland game, he calmly asked longtime executive assistant Gerry Brown to leave the room because he didn't want her to hear the kind of language he was about to use. Then he went off.

"The standards have slipped around here," he yelled, profanities coming about every other word. "We lose to Maryland, and all I hear is 'you guys were one play from winning.' *Bulls*—. We had twenty chances to make that 'one play from winning.' From now on, we're going to play up to *my* [three profanities] standards or heads are going to roll."

As luck would have it, North Carolina was coming to town. Duke hadn't beaten the Tar Heels since 1993—a seven-game losing streak. That afternoon before practice, Krzyzewski showed his players twenty examples of where they could have made a play to win the game the previous day. Then he drew a blue line on the whiteboard and said, "You see this line? You have to tell Carolina that if they want to cross that line, they will have to *kill* you to do it. *Kill* you."

Krzyzewski was angriest at center Greg Newton, who had only had one rebound at Maryland. Not surprisingly, Newton got thrown out of practice that afternoon. Two nights later, Krzyzewski's pregame talk lasted five seconds. He walked into the locker room, drew a blue line on the board, and said, "Let's go."

It wasn't easy, but they didn't let Carolina cross the blue line, hanging on late for an 80–73 win. Capel and Langdon made the key baskets in the final minute, and the students stormed the court for the first time since a 1988 victory over the Tar Heels.

Carolina had also gotten off to a slow start in the ACC, and as Smith and Krzyzewski shook hands, Smith said, "I really think this game will help both teams. You guys deserved to win, but we gave you everything we had."

Smith proved to be prophetic. Duke went on a nine-game winning streak and won the conference with a 12–4 record, finishing one game ahead of Carolina and Wake Forest. The Blue Devils clinched the regular-season title in their second-to-last game by beating Maryland. Knowing his team had a chance to clinch the title, Krzyzewski explained to his players—none of whom had won an ACC championship—why it was so important.

"First of four," Carrawell whispered to fellow freshman Nate James.

Krzyzewski, who heard *everything*, heard the comment.

"Hey," he said pointing at Carrawell, "let's win *one* before we think about four."

As it turned out, Carrawell was only partly right. Duke would win the next *five* regular-season titles.

. . . .

The 1996–97 season, however, didn't end very well. The Blue Devils finished the regular season at North Carolina in what would turn out to be Dean Smith's last home game in the building named in his honor. The Tar Heels won an intense game 91–85. The loss was hardly shocking. Carolina was at least as hot as Duke—Smith had been right about the earlier game in Cameron helping both of them.

But Krzyzewski sensed that something wasn't quite right with his team, the way only a coach can sense when something is amiss. Duke opened the ACC Tournament against eighth-seeded North Carolina State, another team that had played much better in the second half of the season. Under first-year coach Herb Sendek, the Wolfpack had gone 4–4 in the second half of the conference season after starting 0–8.

Prior to the game, while his team was on the court warming up, Krzyzewski restlessly walked around the shower room checking to make sure all the showers had new soap bars in them. When I inquired why in the world he was checking on the soap, he said, "I just have a feeling about this game."

Krzyzewski was right to be concerned. Duke blasted to an early 15-point lead and then looked like it was running in soap suds the rest of the day. State won 66–60 and then upset Maryland the next day in the semifinals before running out of gas against UNC in the championship game. Carolina had started ACC play with a 24-point loss to Wake Forest. In the tournament semifinals, the Tar Heels beat the Deacons 86–73—a 37-point swing from game one to game three (they had also won in Chapel Hill).

The victory in the championship game was Carolina's eleventh straight win and sent them to the East Regional as the top seed. Duke was given a No. 2 seed in the Southeast Regional, and fading Wake Forest was sent west as a No. 3 seed. Only North Carolina made it out of the first weekend.

After the NC State loss, Krzyzewski tried something different. Prior to practice on Monday, he walked his team out to Wallace Wade Stadium, which was where Duke played (often bad) football. In fact, Wallace Wade had once been selected by *Sports Illustrated* as the prettiest place in America to watch bad football.

The stadium was empty, and Krzyzewski had his players sit near the top of the stands on a beautiful March afternoon. "It's spring, guys," he said. "New beginnings, everything fresh. That's where we are right now. We had a great winter, now we start over, and we know we're good enough to do great things. We finished first in a league that sent six teams to the tournament—three of them No. 1 or No. 2 seeds. Let's look at Murray State [Duke's first-round opponent] as the opening game of a new season."

It was certainly an out-of-the-box approach, but Duke still struggled to get past Murray State 82–78, even while playing close to home in Charlotte. Then they ran into Providence, vastly underseeded at No. 10, and were beaten soundly, 98–87. Pete Gillen, the Friars' loquacious coach, talked Saturday as if the Blue Devils were the Michael Jordan Bulls. "They're on TV more than *Leave It to Beaver*!" he declared.

They weren't on TV anymore that season. The Friars ended up reaching the regional final before losing in overtime to Arizona, the eventual national champion.

In the meantime, Tim Duncan's last game at Wake Forest was a 72–66 loss to Stanford, a game that infuriated coach Dave Odom—not because of the loss, but because he was convinced the Stanford big men were allowed to beat Duncan up while the referees appeared to look the other way.

The losses by Wake Forest and Duke left the stage clear for a Carolina coronation. Dean Smith had been closing in on Adolph Rupp's record of 876 wins all season, although the slow start had left people believing he wouldn't break the record until early the following season. But the eleven-game win streak left Smith one game shy of Rupp's record, and he tied it with an easy first-round win over Fairfield in the Lawrence Joel Coliseum, Wake Forest's home court.

In another one of those remarkable NCAA Tournament committee "coincidences," the Tar Heels had been scheduled to play Indiana in the second round. The Hoosiers were coached by Smith's longtime friend and NCAA Tournament nemesis Bob Knight—a perfect Saturday afternoon TV matchup.

Except someone forgot to get the script to Colorado, which routed the Hoosiers 80–56, leaving Knight so angry that he chose to walk the two miles back to the team's hotel—in the snow.

Carolina then easily beat Colorado 73–66 on Saturday, and Smith had win number 877. He had downplayed the whole idea of passing Rupp for several reasons. First, he never liked drawing attention to himself. Second, he wasn't a big fan of Rupp, who he believed was a racist. Rupp didn't recruit a Black player to Kentucky until 1970—four years after his all-white team lost the national championship game to an all-Black Texas Western starting five.

Nowadays, Kentucky people become almost hysterical at any mention of Rupp being a racist. Regardless, Smith believed he was. I know, because he told me so during that 1996–97 season.

But on that Saturday afternoon, Smith was clearly overjoyed, especially because so many former players had come to the game. Terry Holland was chairman of the basketball committee that year, and he left word with the coliseum's security people that VIPs connected with Carolina should be allowed backstage to celebrate with Smith.

Holland and Smith had been longtime antagonists when Holland coached at Virginia. "I did it," Holland said years later about his decision that day, "because it was the right thing to do."

Carolina went on to reach Smith's eleventh Final Four before losing to Arizona in Indianapolis.

A few weeks later, I asked Smith if he would return for a thirty-seventh season. I had been working on a book that winter on ACC basketball and had sensed that he was getting close to the end.

"I'm sixty-six," Smith said. "If you had asked me that question a year ago, I'd have probably said I don't think so. That season wore me out. But I enjoyed coaching this group. We'll see how I feel in October. I certainly won't decide before then."

In October, he decided to retire. He wasn't as excited about the start of practice as he believed he needed to be. On October 9, six days before practice was scheduled to start, he held a press conference in the Dean Dome and announced he was retiring. He teared up only once—when he talked about what his players had meant to him. Many of them had packed the room. Longtime assistant Bill Guthridge, who had worked for Smith for thirty years, was named to replace him.

Guthridge took the Tar Heels to two Final Fours in three seasons, which wasn't good enough for most Carolina fans because he never won a title. After all, think what old Dean Smith could have done with those teams.

Another longtime nemesis sent Smith flowers the day he announced he would no longer coach. The note with the flowers read: "It was an honor to try to compete with you for 17 years. The ACC will never be the same without you." It was signed, "Mike."

Truer words were never spoken.

....

Duke and North Carolina both had excellent seasons in year 1 AD (After Dean).

Krzyzewski was back to where he had once been in recruiting. During the 1996–97 school year, the Blue Devils signed centers Elton Brand and Chris Burgess, swingman Shane Battier, and point guard William Avery. They joined what was now a veteran team that included senior point guard Steve Wojciechowski, Trajan Langdon, Roshown McLeod, and Chris Carrawell.

The Blue Devils spent the entire 1997–98 regular season ranked in the Top 5, reaching No. 1 after beating then No. 1 Arizona in Hawaii in November. They were still No. 1 when they went to Chapel Hill to play No. 2 North Carolina in February and got hammered, 97–73. Their other regular-season loss going into the finale at Cameron had been at Michigan in December. They were 14–1 in the ACC; Carolina was 13–2.

A Duke win would give the Blue Devils the regular-season title for a second straight season; a Carolina win would mean a tie at the top, with UNC getting the top seed in the ACC Tournament after beating Duke twice.

Carolina led the whole afternoon, but Duke rallied late and pulled out a 77–75 win, bringing about a Duke-student court storming for the second straight season. Duke had lost Brand for a month with a broken foot, but he made it back for the Carolina game.

A week later, Carolina easily won the ACC Tournament championship game, giving it two wins in three matchups with Duke. Both teams went into the NCAA Tournament as No. 1 seeds, UNC in the East Regional and Duke in the South Regional.

Carolina made it to the Final Four; Duke did not. The Blue Devils led Kentucky by 17 points in the second half of the regional final but collapsed, unable to keep Kentucky point guard Wayne Turner out of the lane as the lead disappeared. Kentucky won 86–84, finally beating Duke in the NCAA Tournament in the post–"Laettner game" era.

As it turned out, the Tar Heels probably would have been better off not making it to San Antonio. Not only did Carolina lose 65–59 to Utah; the game also turned into arguably the most embarrassing display in the school's long, distinguished history.

Dean Smith had made a recruiting exception three years earlier when he accepted 6-foot-8, 240-pound Makhtar N'Diaye as a transfer from Michigan. N'Diaye had a reputation as a dirty player, but Smith was convinced the "Carolina Way" would change him.

It didn't. N'Diaye was involved in several incidents during the two years he played at Carolina. The worst came in the 1998 Final Four when he spit on Utah's Britten Johnsen. When Johnsen (understandably) complained, N'Diaye denied spitting, then said he'd been responding to a racial slur. In the aftermath, Utah coach Rick Majerus said he would resign on the spot if N'Diaye was telling the truth. Later, N'Diaye—urged to come forward by Bill Guthridge—admitted he'd lied about the racial slur and apologized.

Kentucky beat Utah in the national championship game two nights later, but for most neutrals, the enduring memory of that Final Four would always be N'Diaye's shocking behavior.

. . . .

The 1998–99 season turned out to be one of Mike Krzyzewski's most painful—literally and figuratively.

Duke lost in the Great Alaska Shootout to Cincinnati in November and then won every game it played until April. The Blue Devils were ranked No. 1 almost the entire season and were labeled a "super team" by many. In all, they won thirty-two games in a row, including going 19–0 against ACC teams— 16–0 in the regular season and 3–0 in winning the ACC Tournament—and cruised to their first Final Four since 1994.

The Blue Devils were loaded. Sophomore center Elton Brand was the consensus national player of the year, and fellow sophomore Shane Battier was a star at both ends of the court, as was junior Chris Carrawell. William Avery had stepped into Wojciechowski's point-guard role, and freshman guard Corey Maggette was as good a sixth man as there was in the country.

What many people missed while gushing over Duke was how good Connecticut had become. Like the Blue Devils, the Huskies had lost a year earlier in the Elite Eight and had their key players back, led by shooting guard Richard Hamilton. They were a three-guard team with senior Ricky Moore and sophomore Khalid El-Amin, and they had an excellent big man in Jake Voskuil. UConn came into the tournament with only two losses, one of them in a game in which Voskuil didn't play.

Duke's closest game in the Eastern Regional was a 78–61 Sweet Sixteen win over Southwest Missouri State. The Blue Devils then beat Temple 85–64 to advance to Krzyzewski's eighth Final Four.

Connecticut had a little more trouble in its regional final, beating Gonzaga—which was emerging as a national power—67–62. Both teams then won their semifinals by six over Big Ten teams, Connecticut beating Ohio State and Duke beating Michigan State, the first of Tom Izzo's eight Final Four teams.

That set up a rare final in which the two best teams met. Duke, however, was considered a heavy favorite.

"It was the perfect situation for us," Connecticut coach Jim Calhoun said later. "We knew how good we were, and we also knew the whole world was picking them to win." He smiled. "At least that's what I told the players."

There were two other important factors. Krzyzewski had been struggling with hip issues all winter. It had become a chore for him to walk to and from the court. It wasn't as bad as the back problems, but he was in a lot of pain and had already scheduled hip-replacement surgery for after the season.

The other problem was the matchup between UConn senior Ricky Moore and Duke sophomore William Avery. The two had gone to high school together, and even though Avery had emerged as a star, he still looked up to Moore.

Moore was tougher and more experienced than Avery, and it showed that night. He scored 13 points and had eight rebounds, shooting 6-of-10 from the field. Avery was 3-of-12 from the field and never looked like himself all night.

Maybe if Krzyzewski had gotten in Avery's face and told him he was a better player than Moore and they were not in high school anymore, it would have made a difference. But Krzyzewski could barely stand up. In fact, Quin Snyder, who had become the top assistant after Tommy Amaker left to become the coach at Seton Hall, ran the team most of the night.

Excuse making? Perhaps. Connecticut led most of the second half and won 77–74 when Langdon, who scored 25 points, missed a shot to tie the game in the final seconds. The Huskies were the better team that night, and that was all that mattered. It was the first of six national championships they would win between 1999 and 2024.

The loss was hard to take for the Blue Devils because everyone connected to the team believed it was the better team. It was much like the 1986 team, which also went into the title game with thirty-seven wins only to lose a tight game and fall short of the championship.

"You go from being maybe one of the great teams ever to just another team that played for the championship," said Jay Bilas, recalling his experience on that '86 team. "It's very tough to take, and there's absolutely nothing you can do to change the story for the rest of your life."

Three underclassmen turned pro after the season: Brand, who was the No. 1 pick in the 1999 NBA Draft; Maggette, who was the 13th pick; and Avery, who was the 14th pick. There were those at Duke who thought Maggette was convinced to turn pro by a Sam Smith column in the *Chicago Tribune* quoting NBA scouts as saying Maggette would be the No. 1 pick in the draft. Some thought the column was planted by anti-Duke people who wanted to lure Maggette into the draft. Regardless, Maggette was gone.

The good news was that Krzyzewski had another excellent recruiting class arriving, headlined by Jason Williams, Mike Dunleavy Jr., and Carlos Boozer. They would join with Battier, Carrawell, and Nate James to produce another team that was good enough to contend for the national championship.

Battier was now the unquestioned leader of the team. He knew there would be adjustments to be made in 2000 with three freshman starters, but he also knew the talent level that was there.

"We had two very disappointing losses in '98 and '99," he said. "We let the Kentucky game get away—no excuses, it shouldn't have happened. Then in '99, we were a little beat up from the Michigan State game, but that's not why we lost. We picked a bad night to have a bad game against the wrong team. That one really hurt because we had a chance to be a historic team and we let it get away.

"Then the three guys left. I think [Chris] Carrawell, Nate [James], and I looked around and said, 'Okay, see you later. It's our team now, and we're going to get done what we didn't get done those first two years.'"

The 1999–2000 Blue Devils started poorly, losing to both Stanford and Connecticut in Madison Square Garden as the freshmen settled into their roles. They then went on a 28–2 tear, losing only to Maryland and St. John's, both at home. Battier was the leading scorer, but Carrawell was the ACC player of the year. They went 15–1 in ACC play, giving Carrawell four straight ACC regular-season titles. Then they beat Maryland in the ACC Tournament championship game for their second straight tournament title.

The Blue Devils were again the No. 1 seed in the East Regional and had to win a difficult second-round game against Kansas. The Jayhawks were having a relatively down year, having finished 23–9, and as a result they were a No. 8 seed.

During the game, Krzyzewski and Roy Williams got into a shouting match, bringing back memories of Krzyzewski–Dean Smith duels. Billy Packer took note of that fact, commenting, "I don't think this has anything to do with Duke and Kansas, I think it has to do with the color blue—light blue versus dark blue."

Duke won 69–64 and went to Syracuse to play a Sweet Sixteen game against Billy Donovan's first very good Florida team. The Gators pulled away late to win 87–78. The loss brought a thud-like ending to what had been a surprisingly good season.

"It was tough to take," Mike Dunleavy said. "I mean, we'd lost two games in four months, and we were a number-one seed. We really thought we were good enough to win it all."

Being good enough to win it all is different than actually winning it all. Duke had now learned that difficult lesson in three straight seasons.

"The Florida game gave us an edge going into the next season," Battier said. "It was my last chance, and I didn't want to walk away without winning a championship. I couldn't even bear the thought."

In February 2001, Duke held a ten-year-reunion for the 1991 championship team. After the game, in the locker room, as Battier brought his team together, he noticed Laettner, Hurley, Davis, Koubek, and some of their teammates lingering outside the circle.

"Hey '91, get up here," he said.

As the championship-team players joined the circle, Battier pointed at his teammates and said, "Now, we have to do what they did."

5

. . . .

BANNER THREE ...
FINALLY

The only player of note to leave after the 1999–2000 season was Chris Carrawell, who graduated. Freshman Chris Duhon, a dynamic combination
guard from Louisiana, was added to a talented, experienced group.

"We were shaken up by the Florida loss," Mike Dunleavy Jr. said. "We
were young that year, but also old. Jason [Williams] and Carlos [Boozer]
were more ready to play than I was. But I had time to adapt because they were
ready, and Battier, James, and Carrawell were very ready. But Florida was
good—probably better than we'd thought. If Mike Miller doesn't hit the

shot at the buzzer, they lose in the first round to Butler. We thought we were better than they were. We were wrong."

Williams, Boozer, and Dunleavy—now sophomores—joined Battier and James in the starting lineup. The only player who saw serious minutes off the bench was Duhon. Krzyzewski was always a believer in a short bench. He might start the season playing nine or even ten players, but by the time conference play rolled around, he had usually settled on a seven-man rotation. In this case, he had a six-man rotation, with others spotting in when needed because of foul trouble or at the end of a blowout.

The Blue Devils were never ranked lower than third the entire season. They began by winning the preseason NIT in Madison Square Garden and were unbeaten until they traveled to Oakland to play Stanford in late December. The Cardinal, who had always given Duke trouble, won the game 84–83, dropping Duke to 10–1 and to No. 3 in the national polls.

Five weeks later, having won eight in a row, they traveled to Cole Field House to play eighth-ranked Maryland. By this time, Gary Williams had rebuilt Maryland into a national power, although he had not yet reached the Final Four.

To Williams and the Terrapins, Duke had become Mount Everest. Maryland was able to beat North Carolina on a semiregular basis but didn't have that kind of luck against Duke. Going into the 2000–2001 season, Williams was 3–21 against Krzyzewski since he had arrived to take over a wounded program in College Park.

The Terrapins had beaten Duke in Cameron the previous season, the Blue Devils' lone ACC regular-season loss. But when the two teams met in a rematch in the ACC Tournament final, Duke won easily, 81–68. As the nets were coming down, longtime Maryland radio play-by-play man Johnny Holliday probably summed up the way Maryland people felt when he said, "I can't think of a worse way to spend a Sunday afternoon than sitting here watching Duke cut down the nets."

Maryland returned a great backcourt the next season: Juan Dixon and Steve Blake. The Terrapins also had a talented big man in Lonny Baxter and a rapidly improving inside presence in Chris Wilcox. Like Duke, the Terrapins were loaded.

Remarkably, even though Williams had taken over a team saddled with two years of NCAA sanctions because of violations under his predecessor, Bob

Wade, and was now on his way to an eighth-straight NCAA Tournament appearance, Maryland fans and alumni were restless. They began referring to Williams as a "Sweet Sixteen" coach, referencing his four Sweet Sixteen appearances that had all resulted in losses in that round. One group of alumni was pushing hard for Maryland to hire Mike Brey, who'd had great success up the road at Delaware and had grown up a few miles from Maryland's campus.

Fortunately for them, that scenario never played out.

. . . .

The season hadn't started well for Maryland. They had lost twice in Maui and then on the road at Wisconsin. They'd also lost a home game to North Carolina—never a shock, but disappointing.

The Terrapins were 11–4 when Duke came to Cole Field House on January 27—the night before the Baltimore Ravens were scheduled to play the New York Giants in the Super Bowl. Maryland was the better team for 39 minutes and had a 10-point lead with 60 seconds to play. Cole was going nuts; the only time in Williams's eleven seasons that Maryland had beaten Duke at home had been in 1995, the year Pete Gaudet was Duke's coach for all but one ACC game.

"Maryland fans have waited for this for a long time," Maryland grad Len Elmore said on TV with a minute to go as the students prepared to rush the court.

It never happened. With Steve Blake having fouled out, Jason Williams made two steals and hit two threes in the final minute of regulation, and the game went into overtime. Duke won 98–96, and the scene went from celebratory to ugly as frustrated Maryland fans lobbed things at the court. Duke alum Mark Alarie was at the game and was hit with a plastic water bottle as he tried to leave with his infant daughter in his arms.

To this day, Maryland fans insist that the officials stole the game. Duke people simply refer to it as the "Miracle Minute."

"It was great to win the game that way," Jason Williams said years later. "What we didn't really understand that night was how important the game would turn out to be. After what had happened there, we never thought we could lose to them. It wasn't that they weren't good—they were very good—we just believed if it was close, we were going to win the game. We knew them, they knew us. They knew we were never done."

Five nights later, Duke lost at home to North Carolina. The Tar Heels were coached by Matt Doherty and had become one of the better stories of the season. Bill Guthridge had retired after going to two Final Fours in three seasons, having grown weary of UNC fans who desperately wanted Roy Williams to come home and lead the team to glory.

Williams would eventually do that, but when Dean Smith called him after Guthridge stepped down, Williams couldn't bring himself to take the job. He'd been to two Final Fours at Kansas but hadn't won a national championship.

"Most difficult conversation of my life," he said years later. "Can you imagine me saying no to Coach Smith? Impossible. But I really felt I hadn't yet finished the job at Kansas."

Williams's decision was understandable. He was still a young coach at fifty, and he felt a commitment to Kansas, which had given him his first head-coaching job. He made one mistake: during his press conference announcing he was staying, Williams said he would be at Kansas "forever." Kansas fans believed him, and when "forever" became only three more seasons, he was never forgiven.

Doherty, who had played on Carolina's 1982 national championship team and been the head coach at Notre Dame for one season, got the job after both Larry Brown and Eddie Fogler also turned it down.

The Tar Heels came to Cameron ranked fourth in the country and stunned Duke 85–83. Four weeks later, on Senior Night against Maryland, Carlos Boozer went down with a broken right foot with just under 10 minutes left and Duke leading 64–60. As soon as Boozer left, Maryland, more than eager to make up for the "Miracle Minute," went on a 14–2 run, hit all its free throws in the final minutes, and beat the Blue Devils 91–80.

....

What was more important was the prospect of playing without Boozer for up to a month. The possibility that Duke's season might be over before Boozer was healthy enough to play was quite real.

The starting center for the game that Sunday at North Carolina would be 6-11 sophomore Casey Sanders, who was averaging 2.5 points per game. Nick Horvath, Matt Christensen, and football walk-on Reggie Love would back him up. The four of them combined didn't average as many points or rebounds as Boozer.

Which is why Krzyzewski decided that the last day of February was a good day to completely scrap his offense and start all over again in preparing for the thirtieth game of the season.

"He walked into the locker room the next day and said, 'If you f—ing play the way I want you to play, we're beating Carolina on Sunday,'" Battier said. "It wasn't anything rah-rah or a pep talk, it was completely factual. And then he told us how we're going to do it."

As always after a game, Krzyzewski had been up most of the night after the Maryland loss. But the postmidnight meeting with his coaches hadn't just been about breaking down the game tape. It had been about deciding what to do without Boozer. They would have to play differently with four different centers who were not scorers. Or perhaps they could play without a center?

In the end, they decided that Casey Sanders, the most athletic of the four big men available, would start at center. Chris Duhon would move into the starting lineup at point guard, and Jason Williams would move to shooting guard. Nate James would come off the bench to play big guard or small forward, depending on the circumstances. It would be a six-man rotation, and four of the six players getting major minutes were very good three-point shooters: Duhon, Williams, Dunleavy, and Battier. Occasionally, Duke would play without a pure center, putting Battier on the other team's big man.

The emphasis would be on three-point shooting. If the ball went inside, it was with the intention of having it passed back outside. Sanders, Christensen, and Love combined to play 27 minutes against UNC and took only one shot among them. As a team, the Blue Devils took 72 shots—38 of them from outside the three-point line.

"If you think about it, what Coach K did was apply analytics to the situation when no one—including him—really knew what analytics were," Battier said. "Overnight, literally overnight, he came up with an offense that, statistically speaking, needed to shoot as many threes as possible."

Analytics, in one form or another, had been around for a long time and had been applied to baseball by Bill James in his annual books. But no one in power really used them until Billy Beane's 2002 Oakland Athletics. Beane and analytics became famous after that season thanks to Michael Lewis's book *Moneyball*, which became a movie starring Brad Pitt in 2011.

When Krzyzewski redesigned his offense prior to going to Chapel Hill on March 2, 2001, almost no one in sports had ever heard the term "analytics."

Regardless of the terminology, Duke played a near-perfect game against the Tar Heels, winning 95–81. (Jason Williams scored 33 points; Shane Battier added 25.) The teams tied for the ACC regular-season title, although UNC was the No. 1 seed in the tournament, played that year in Atlanta's Georgia Dome.

The seeding hardly seemed to matter—except that Duke would have to play No. 3 seed Maryland in the ACC Tournament semifinals. The game was back and forth all afternoon. Maryland overcame a 14-point deficit to tie the game at 82 on a Blake three-pointer, but James tipped in Williams's missed jumper with 1.3 seconds to go.

There was still enough time for Maryland to get off a shot, but Juan Dixon's thirty-five-footer hit the back rim as the buzzer sounded, and Duke hung on to win 74–72. The next day, Duke and Carolina met in the ACC Tournament final. Duke was even more dominant than it had been a week earlier, winning 79–53. The win meant that Duke finished the regular season with a record of 29–4 and was awarded the No. 1 seed in the East Regional, while North Carolina was sent to the South Regional as the No. 2 seed.

Maryland was sent west as a No. 3 seed. The Terrapins had to face a greatly underseeded George Mason team in the first round and easily could have lost to the Patriots. With Maryland leading 81–80 and the clock under five seconds, Mason center George Evans appeared to have Lonny Baxter sealed in the low post. But the pass went under Baxter's hands and out-of-bounds, and Maryland got the 83–80 win.

In a twist, Maryland's next opponent wasn't sixth-seeded Wisconsin as expected but 11th-seeded Georgia State, coached by Lefty Driesell. The Panthers had stunned Wisconsin 50–49. When Driesell was asked after the game how life was different coaching at a mid-major like Georgia State as opposed to a power school like Maryland, he responded as only he could.

"Mid-major?" he exclaimed. "Mid-major? I ain't never been mid-anything. Go ask Wisconsin if we're mid-major."

Driesell's team may not have been a mid-major in his mind, but it wasn't good enough to compete with Maryland two days later, losing to the Terrapins 69–50. Maryland then cruised past another surprise team, 10th-seeded Georgetown (two D.C.-area teams playing in Anaheim, California), and then easily beat top-seeded Stanford in the regional final to make it to the Final Four.

Suddenly, Gary Williams was no longer just a Sweet Sixteen coach. And that summer, Mike Brey left Delaware for Notre Dame, where he eventually would become the school's winningest coach ever. A happy ending for all.

North Carolina's season did not have a happy ending. After easily beating Princeton in the first round, the Tar Heels were upset by Penn State. They had gone from one of the season's better stories to one of the tournament's early upsets.

Ten days later, Matt Doherty was chosen as the Associated Press coach of the year. As with most awards, the ballots had to be submitted by the end of the regular season. This led Mike Shalin, the *Boston Herald*'s very clever columnist, to write: "Matt Doherty, who guided North Carolina from a Final Four berth a year ago to a second-round NCAA tournament defeat this year, was today chosen as the AP's college basketball coach of the year."

. . . .

The second seed in the East behind Duke was (surprise!) Kentucky. The East Regional was scheduled to be played in (surprise again!) Philadelphia, although the Spectrum had closed and had been replaced by what was then called the First Union Center. The building was right across the parking lot from the Spectrum.

The NCAA and CBS did not, however, get their Duke-Kentucky Philadelphia rematch. These weren't the Rocky movies—you couldn't script them.

The Blue Devils had a tough second-round game in Greensboro against Missouri. Quin Snyder had left Duke to become the coach at Missouri, and his team hung with the Blue Devils for 35 minutes. Both coaches admitted afterward that it had been difficult to coach against the other, especially with so much at stake. Duke finally pulled away late to win 94–81. That put the Blue Devils in Philadelphia in a round of 16 game against UCLA. Meanwhile, sixth-seeded Southern California (USC) had upset third-seeded Boston College to advance to a matchup with Kentucky.

Duke upheld its end of the bargain by beating UCLA 76–63, but Henry Bibby's USC team messed with the TV ratings by upsetting Kentucky. The Wildcats really weren't that good—they'd been lucky to survive a first-round matchup against Holy Cross, coached by former Kentucky assistant Ralph Willard.

Duke played USC for a spot in the Final Four and won 79–69. Two years earlier, the Blue Devils had decided not to cut down the nets after winning the East Regional because the net they really wanted was the one that would come down eight days later in St. Petersburg.

But Connecticut had cut down that net. This time, Krzyzewski told his players to cut the net down.

"We aren't going to make that mistake again," Krzyzewski said. "We're going to enjoy this. We'll worry about next week, next week."

Boozer was able to come back and play in Philadelphia, although he was still clearly limited. He played 21 minutes against UCLA and 22 minutes against USC, but he didn't score much—three points total in the two games. He was a presence on defense, however, and allowed Sanders to rest and be fresh when he was in the game.

Krzyzewski was glad to have Boozer back, but he knew his team would need more from him if it was going to beat Maryland in Minneapolis. He wasn't about to change his starting lineup since Duke had won six straight games with Sanders as the starter at center.

If TV hadn't gotten what it wanted in the regionals, it certainly had ideal matchups for the national semifinals. In the first game, Michigan State—in the Final Four for a third straight season and trying to go back-to-back as national champions—would play Arizona. Bobbi Olson, who had been married to Arizona coach Lute Olson for forty-seven years, had died of ovarian cancer in January, making Olson's Wildcats the sentimental favorite in Minneapolis.

Game two would be the fourth matchup of the season between Duke and Maryland. Each of the first three games had been wild in a different way: Duke's "Miracle Minute"; Maryland's revenge and Boozer's injury, which had changed Duke's season; and James's tip-in for the Duke win in the ACC Tournament semifinals.

"What was great about those three games is that both teams played well in all of them," Maryland coach Gary Williams said prior to the game. "There's no one we respect more than Duke, but the first three games have proven to us that we can certainly compete with them."

After Arizona had pulled away from Michigan State to win the first game, Duke and Maryland took the floor to play one another for the fourth time in nine weeks. For most of the first half, it appeared that the question was whether the Blue Devils could compete with the Terrapins.

"The Final Four is very different than any other basketball game," Battier said. "You're playing in a dome, and the shooting background is completely different. It's just . . . weird. You feel for a while like you're playing in a starship. It also *feels* different because walking onto the floor in a building that big with that many people in it is unlike anything else you've experienced.

"If you look back, it isn't that unusual for one team, or even both teams, to really lay an egg early. Unfortunately, it was us. I was the only guy on the floor who had played in a Final Four before, and I wasn't any good, either."

None of the Maryland players had been in a Final Four, either, but they appeared completely unbothered by the unique atmosphere. They came out hot—notably Juan Dixon—and looked as if they might run Duke out of the building before halftime.

The Terrapins built their lead to 39–17 with three-fourths of the building roaring. Duke had become college basketball's Darth Vader by now, and the Michigan State and Arizona fans loved the idea that Duke might get humiliated. At that point, Duke was 0-of-8 from the three-point line, and Maryland was 5-of-6.

With 6:22 left, Krzyzewski called a rare first-half time-out. The players all remembered those two minutes vividly.

"He didn't go crazy or anything," Battier said. "In fact, he was very calm. He said, 'Fellas, it doesn't matter if we lose by thirty or by sixty. What matters is, if we go out, that we do it being ourselves. We aren't ourselves right now. We're letting them dictate everything. Just play basketball. That's all I ask.'"

Krzyzewski also made a couple of moves that proved important: he put Nate James in the game to give the cold-shooting Mike Dunleavy a breather. And he told Carlos Boozer he had to be more aggressive on offense. The time when the Blue Devils could play four-on-five on offense had long since passed.

James promptly hit a three-point shot from the corner to, if not stop the bleeding, stanch it a bit. The defense picked up, and Boozer began to find space inside on offense, surprising the Terrapins with his aggressiveness.

"Nate's shot may have been the most important shot anyone hit in my four years," Battier said. "It was as if we got our balance back right there."

Jason Williams agrees. "I'm not sure Nate ever got the credit he deserved for us winning that championship," he said. "Think about it, he's a senior and he's replaced in the starting lineup by a freshman [Duhon]. He doesn't pout or complain, he says, 'Okay, how do I help us win coming off the bench?' And he did exactly that."

By halftime, the lead was down to 49–38. It had been 46–38 until Dixon hit a three just prior to the buzzer to put the lead back into double digits. "They were up eleven, but they were the ones who were yelling at each other going off the court," Battier said. "I wasn't thinking 'we've got them,' but I was certainly thinking 'we *can* get them.'"

All the Duke players remembered what the score was when Krzyzewski called the time-out, if only because they'd never faced a deficit like that in their lives.

"If you think about it, 39–17, that's a *lot* of points," Dunleavy said. "But there was also a lot of time left. I suppose we could have panicked and gotten blown out, but we were calm. Coach K was calm. And once we started to get close to them, we felt like we had them."

Krzyzewski made two more adjustments at halftime. First, he took the ball completely out of Williams's hands, telling him not to help Duhon with ballhandling or running the offense. Second, and perhaps more important, he put the 6-6 James in the game to guard the 6-1 Dixon.

Maryland's star had 16 points at halftime and seemed able to get his shot whenever he wanted or needed one. In the second half, with James chasing him all over the floor, Dixon took only two shots, making one. James guarding Dixon did another important thing: it made life easier for Williams at the defensive end of the court, allowing him to focus on finding his own shot on offense.

After starting the game "feeling as if I was shooting with my eyes closed," Williams was able to open his eyes and, with his three-point shot not falling, begin getting into the lane to score. Boozer was also a force. At the defensive end, he held Lonny Baxter to 2-of-10 shooting and muscled his way inside to score 19 points on 7-of-8 shooting. Duhon ran the offense with cold efficiency, scoring 10 points, adding six assists, and turning the ball over only twice in 33 minutes.

But it was the two seniors, Battier and James, who were ultimately the heroes. Battier was Battier, scoring 25 points, grabbing eight rebounds, and handling the ball late against Maryland's pressure. He also made all his key free throws down the stretch.

James had nine points and nine rebounds, but it was the invisible stat—his defense on Dixon—that made the difference in the game.

Duke took the lead 73–72 with 6:28 to play on the only three-pointer Williams made all day (he finished 1-of-9), and even though the game stayed close until the last couple of minutes, the Blue Devils always had the answer for anything Maryland threw at them.

Boozer put them ahead for good by sinking two free throws to make it 78–77 with 4:43 left. Maryland was finally out of gas. The Blue Devils outscored them 17–7 the rest of the way, and the final margin was a deceiving 95–84. What wasn't deceiving was this: from the time Krzyzewski called time-out in the first half until the final buzzer, Duke outscored Maryland 78–45.

That remarkable margin made the inevitable Maryland complaints about the officiating pretty hollow. Most Maryland fans believe the Terrapins have never been beaten fair and square by anyone, especially Duke. North Carolina State fans share the same sort of paranoia, especially when playing Duke or North Carolina.

Krzyzewski was once asked what happens when Maryland plays NC State, since *neither* school ever got a fair whistle.

"There's a lot of angst," he answered.

There was plenty of angst on the Maryland side and plenty of joy on the Duke side after this game. It wasn't just the fourth time these two teams had clashed that season; it was in the Final Four—Maryland's first appearance ever. Their fans had gone from dancing in the aisles (literally) in the first half to screaming to the heavens (literally and loudly) at game's end.

. . . .

Duke's victory set up a national championship game with Arizona, the third meeting between the teams since the 1989 game in which Christian Laettner's missed free throw had proved to be the last time he'd ever miss a clutch shot. Duke had won at home in 1990, Arizona had won at home the following season, and Arizona had won in Hawaii in 1997. The two teams had never met in an NCAA Tournament game, much less a game that would decide the national champion.

Arizona had an experienced and loaded roster, led by two superb guards, Gilbert Arenas and Jason Gardner. They also had future NBA star Richard Jefferson and 7-foot-1 Loren Woods, who had transferred from Wake Forest.

Unlike the Maryland game, neither team got off to a quick start. What was apparent early was that Duke was *really* playing a road game. On Saturday, the Arizona and Michigan State fans had clearly been rooting for Maryland, but not with any real passion. Now, in addition to the fervor of the Arizona fans, Duke had to deal with the still very angry Maryland fans, who screamed—often louder than the Arizona fans—whenever a call went in Duke's favor.

"I remember thinking if the fans had their way, I'd already be fouled out," said Jason Williams, who had to go to the bench with two fouls in the first half—about ten fewer than the crowd thought he had actually committed. "I was definitely guarding Gilbert [Arenas] as tightly as I could. If I breathed on him, it felt like the crowd wanted a foul."

Even with Williams on the bench for eight minutes, Duke managed to make it to halftime with a 35–33 lead. The lead was 39–37 early in the second half, when Mike Dunleavy found a phone booth somewhere and emerged as Superman.

"I hadn't shot well for most of the tournament," he said later. "I guess I was due."

Dunleavy had been 1-of-7 at halftime, totaling three points. Suddenly, during a 90-second spurt, everything changed.

He hit a three-pointer out of the half-court offense to make it 42–37. "I heard Coach K yelling from the bench, 'Shoot, shoot!'" Dunleavy said. "I told him later that I was going to shoot anyway."

A moment later, Dunleavy came open in transition and fired and made

Duke's Tommy Amaker cuts down the ACC Tournament championship nets in the Greensboro Coliseum, March 9, 1986. The Blue Devils outlasted Georgia Tech 68–67 to give Duke coach Mike Krzyzewski the first of his fifteen conference tournament titles.

Photo by Chuck Liddy/The Herald-Sun

BELOW. The 1986–87 Blue Devils, an important "bridge" team that led to Duke's subsequent five straight Final Four appearances. Key contributors that season included seniors Tommy Amaker (4) and Martin Nessley (51); juniors Billy King (55) and Kevin Strickland (31); sophomores Danny Ferry (35), Quin Snyder (14), and John Smith (33); and freshmen Phil Henderson (44) and Alaa Abdelnaby (30).

Photo courtesy of the David M. Rubenstein Rare Book & Manuscript Library, Duke University

OPPOSITE. Brian Davis (*left*) and Christian Laettner sense victory near game's end as Duke upset the highly favored, undefeated, and defending champion UNLV Runnin' Rebels 79–77 in the NCAA semifinals in Indianapolis's RCA Dome, March 30, 1991. Two nights later against Kansas, the Blue Devils won the national title—head coach Mike Krzyzewski's first and the first in Duke men's basketball history.

Photo by Chuck Liddy/The Herald-Sun

OPPOSITE. Intensity is written on the faces of Duke team leaders Bobby Hurley (*left*) and Grant Hill at a practice during the 1992 NCAA East Regionals in the Philadelphia Spectrum.

ABOVE. Players and coaches watch anxiously from the Duke bench moments before Grant Hill's 75-foot pass to Christian Laettner in the closing seconds of the East Regional finals against Kentucky in the Spectrum in Philadelphia, March 28, 1992. The top-seeded and defending national champion Blue Devils trailed the second-seeded Wildcats 103–102 with 2.1 seconds remaining in overtime. Laettner caught Hill's pass and made the shot as time expired, winning the game and propelling the Blue Devils to the Final Four in Minneapolis, where they captured their second NCAA national championship.

Photos by Chuck Liddy/The Herald-Sun

Coach Mike Krzyzewski raises the victory net after
Duke stunned Kentucky 104–103 on Christian
Laettner's last-second shot in the NCAA East
Regional finals in the Philadelphia Spectrum,
March 28, 1992. Brian Davis (*arms raised*),
Laettner (*far right*), and their teammates celebrate
the win with their coach. The shot by Laettner is
widely considered one of the greatest moments in
sports history.

Photo by Chuck Liddy/The Herald-Sun

Shane Battier handles the ball during a home game against rival North Carolina as Julius Peppers defends. In Battier's four seasons at Duke (1997–2001), his teams went 8–3 against the Tar Heels and 16–3 in the NCAA Tournament, including winning the national championship his senior year.

Photo by Chuck Liddy/The News & Observer

Coach Mike Krzyzewski hugs Shane Battier as
they, Mike Dunleavy Jr., and Carlos Boozer watch
a highlight video in Minneapolis's Metrodome
following the trophy presentation for the Blue
Devils' 82–72 win over Arizona in the NCAA
national championship game, April 2, 2001.

Photo by Chuck Liddy/The News & Observer

BELOW LEFT. Chris Duhon (2000–2004) ranks first among Duke's all-time career leaders in steals (301) and second in assists (819), trailing only Bobby Hurley (1,076).

BELOW RIGHT. J. J. Redick (2002–2006) ended his Duke career as the leading scorer in ACC history (2,769 points) and the NCAA record holder in three-point field goals (457).

Photos courtesy of the David M. Rubenstein Rare Book & Manuscript Library, Duke University

OPPOSITE, TOP. Coach Mike Krzyzewski diagrams a play during a first-half time-out at Cameron Indoor Stadium in Durham, November 5, 2008.

OPPOSITE, BOTTOM. Coach Mike Krzyzewski directs his players in the closing seconds of Duke's game against Florida State at Cameron Indoor Stadium in Durham, March 3, 2009. The Blue Devils prevailed over the Seminoles, 84–81.

BELOW. Duke coaches Chris Collins, Mike Krzyzewski, and Steve Wojciechowski try to get the attention of players on the court during the Blue Devils' 64–54 win over the North Carolina Tar Heels in the Dean E. Smith Center in Chapel Hill, February 10, 2010.

Photos by Chuck Liddy/The News & Observer

Duke's Jon Scheyer takes an off-balance shot that drops in as he is fouled by a Butler player in the second half of the NCAA national championship game in Lucas Oil Stadium in Indianapolis, April 5, 2010. Scheyer finished with 15 points for the victorious Blue Devils.

Photo by Chuck Liddy/The News & Observer

Captions on next page.

PREVIOUS PAGE, TOP. Duke players and coaches are all smiles as they watch a video of Final Four highlights on the big screen in Indianapolis's Lucas Oil Stadium after defeating Butler 61–59 in the NCAA national championship game, April 5, 2010.

PREVIOUS PAGE, BOTTOM. Coach Mike Krzyzewski shakes hands with North Carolina head coach Roy Williams following Duke's 79–73 win over the Tar Heels at Cameron Indoor Stadium in Durham, February 9, 2011. A gaggle of photographers document the moment.

Photos by Chuck Liddy/The News & Observer

OPPOSITE. Duke coach Mike Krzyzewski talks
with players Rodney Hood (5), Quinn Cook (2),
Jabari Parker (1), and Tyler Thornton (3) before
his team inbounds the ball with less than a minute
remaining in the ACC Tournament semifinal game
against NC State in the Greensboro Coliseum,
March 15, 2014. Duke won 75–67 and went on to
face Virginia in the championship game.

ABOVE. Coach K stands with (*left to right*)
Grayson Allen, Quinn Cook, and Justise Winslow
as they watch the "One Shining Moment" video
after the Blue Devils defeated the Wisconsin
Badgers 68–63 in the NCAA national championship game in Indianapolis's Lucas Oil Stadium,
April 6, 2015.

Photos by Chuck Liddy/The News & Observer

Duke coach Mike Krzyzewski walks onto the
court before a home game at Cameron Indoor
Stadium with the Blue Devils' five national
championship banners hanging in the background.
Krzyzewski is the winningest men's head coach
in NCAA Division I basketball history with 1,202
victories.

Photo by Chuck Liddy/The News & Observer

another three, this one from the left side—out of the range of Krzyzew-ski's voice in what had become a loud building, especially behind the Duke bench, where the Duke fans were located.

Loren Woods, who would finish with 22 points and 11 rebounds for Arizona, scored inside, but Dunleavy promptly hit another three. A Carlos Boozer basket made the run 11–2, and Duke had a 50–39 lead.

But the game, as the TV announcers like to say, was long from over. Boozer was being asked to play more minutes than he'd played in a game since the foot injury—he ended up logging 30 minutes—and was struggling against Woods and Arizona's other big man, Richard Jefferson. The two combined on a quick 9–0 Arizona run, and it was 50–48.

Krzyzewski called time. He decided to gamble and give Boozer a breather. That meant that Battier had to guard Woods, who was five inches taller and considerably heavier than he was.

"My best chance, maybe my only chance, was to front him and try to deny him the ball," Battier said. "It didn't work all the time, but it worked just enough."

Duke was trying desperately to keep Arizona at arm's length, but the Wildcats wouldn't go away. Battier played all 40 minutes and had 18 points, 11 rebounds, and six assists. Duhon played 39 minutes. Williams was limited to 29 minutes by foul trouble, but that proved to be enough. Dunleavy shot 7-of-10 in the second half to finish with 21 points, his nine points in 90 seconds being the most important of his college career.

Twice in the last four minutes, Arizona cut the lead to three. Both times, Battier grabbed offensive rebounds and scored. "His outside shot wasn't there," Krzyzewski said about Battier after the game. "But he still found a way down the stretch to make big plays."

Olson agreed. "With Duke, you're never sure who is going to get hot," he said. "The one thing you can be sure of is that Battier's going to be great. There's a reason why he deserved to be the national player of the year."

Williams tossed a perfect lob pass to Battier with a little more than two minutes to go to make the score 77–72. A moment later, he came off a high Battier screen and drilled a three-pointer to make it 80–72. That, as it turned out, was the dagger.

"I couldn't find my three-point shot all weekend," said Williams, who went 3-of-20 in Minneapolis. "But Shane finally got me an open look, and it went in. Talk about breathing a sigh of relief. I remember when that went in thinking, 'We've got 'em, we've finally got 'em.'"

They did have them. The final was 82–72, and the hugging began.

"I remember with a couple of seconds left, Chris [Duhon] had the ball, and he handed it to me," Williams said. "He said, 'Here, you deserve to have this.' The clock hit zero, and I threw the ball as high in the air as I possibly could. It was an amazing feeling." He paused. "I'm not sure it's come down yet."

There's a famous photo of Battier and Krzyzewski locked in an embrace, one that everyone remembered going on seemingly forever. But Williams remembered getting to Battier first. "I headed straight to him, hugged him, and said, 'You're the greatest leader I've ever played with,'" he said. "It felt like the absolute right thing to do."

As the nets were coming down, Battier found his parents. The Duke students' favorite chant when Battier shut down an opponent's scorer had become "Who's your daddy? Battier!"

"My dad loved that chant," Battier said. "Someone made up a shirt for him that said, 'I'm your daddy Battier.' He loved that shirt, and he was wearing it that night. He passed away three years ago. I like to think about him in that shirt in that moment. It's a great memory."

In his final TV interview as a Duke player, Battier smiled and said, "We finally got it done. Now all I have to do is ride off on a white horse."

For Krzyzewski, the victory was especially gratifying because he'd traveled from the nadir of 1995, when he was prepared to resign, to the zenith of a third national championship. It meant that only John Wooden, with an unreachable ten NCAA titles, and Adolph Rupp, with four, had won more national championships than he had. And he had matched Bob Knight, his onetime mentor, with three.

. . . .

There were, as always, amusing sidebars to Duke's national championship run. One such sidebar involved Ron Green Jr., a columnist for the *Charlotte Observer*, whose father and wife were both North Carolina graduates. Green wasn't covering the Final Four that year because he had to be in Augusta, Georgia, early Tuesday morning to cover the Masters. His wife,

Tamara, was (is) one of the many Carolina fans who believe that Mike Krzyzewski is the devil. Which is why she refused to watch the championship game that night with her husband, who had covered and was fond of Krzyzewski.

When Ron came to bed after the game was over, Tamara sleepily asked him who had won.

"Duke," he answered.

"Oh, no," she groaned. "Now we'll have to hear from all the Duke people that Krzyzewski has won as many national titles as Coach Smith."

"No," Ron said. "You won't have to hear that."

"Why not?"

"Because Mike's got three now. Dean had two."

Not as funny as that, perhaps, but more important in an entirely different way was a story that arose from Krzyzewski's election to the Naismith Basketball Hall of Fame—which actually had been announced before he'd won his third national title.

Soon after returning home from Minneapolis, Krzyzewski called Knight and insisted he come to the phone (neither man owned a cell phone at that point). They hadn't spoken a full sentence to one another since the 1992 Final Four.

"Coach," Krzyzewski said. "Please hear me out on this. I'm not even sure at this point what you and I have been angry about for nine years. But one thing I do know for sure is this: if I hadn't played for you and coached for you, I wouldn't be going into the hall of fame. You are the only person who should give my induction speech."

Even Knight couldn't resist that request.

"Mike," he said. "I'd be honored."

Feud ended. At least for a while.

6

. . . .

THE SECOND DROUGHT

There was reason to believe that Duke could repeat in 2002 the same way it had repeated in 1992.

Two key players had graduated: Shane Battier and Nate James. Two players had arrived to try and take up the slack: freshman guard Daniel Ewing and 6-foot-6 junior forward Dahntay Jones, a transfer from Rutgers.

More important, Jason Williams, Carlos Boozer, and Mike Dunleavy had all returned for their junior seasons, and Chris Duhon was now established at the point-guard spot. Duke was an experienced team that knew how to win; the 2001 championship banner hanging next to the title banners from 1991 and 1992 in Cameron was emphatic proof of that.

The national title was the climax of a remarkable resurgence by Krzyzewski. Duke had now won at least thirty games in four straight seasons and had also won the ACC Tournament three straight seasons. In 1997, after the first-round tournament loss to NC State, Duke basketball historian Al Featherston wrote, "If Krzyzewski's resume has a weakness, it is the ACC Tournament, which he has now won three times in his 17 seasons."

As usual with Krzyzewski's weaknesses, that one had been corrected.

Maryland had returned all its key players from the 2001 Final Four team and was clearly on a mission after blowing the 22-point lead in Minneapolis. Kansas hadn't been to a Final Four since 1993 but also had a veteran team returning from a relatively down season—26–7 with a Sweet Sixteen loss to Illinois in March.

Duke began the season by winning the Maui Classic and cruised through its nonconference schedule with a 12–0 record, winning most games by wide margins. The first loss was a stunner: the Blue Devils fell at Florida State 77–76.

During his last two years at Duke, when his teams were often ranked No. 1, Bill Foster had made the comment that you really knew you had arrived as a program when an opponent's students stormed the court after beating you. Krzyzewski's teams were now treated to court stormings whenever they lost on the road.

Fortunately for the Blue Devils, there were only two more court stormings during the 2001–2 regular season: at Maryland and at Virginia. Duke finished the regular season with a record of 26–3, which included two routs of North Carolina.

Matt Doherty's Tar Heels had fallen on remarkably hard times. They lost to Duke 87–58 *at home* and at Maryland 112–79. They finished 8–20, the worst record in school history, and lost meekly to Duke in the first round of the ACC Tournament. Carolina was so bad that the 60–48 loss to the Blue Devils in their third meeting of the season was seen by some as a moral victory.

. . . .

Duke went on to win the ACC Tournament for a fourth straight season and was a No. 1 NCAA Tournament seed for a fifth straight season.

They won a tough second-round game against a Mike Brey–coached Notre Dame team—a loss Brey took very hard. When I called him the next week, Brey didn't call back, which was completely out of character. When he did call back, he said, "I'm sorry it took me a while to get back. I just couldn't talk to anyone connected to Duke for a few days."

Duke moved on to Rupp Arena, where the South Regional semifinals and finals were being played. Maryland had tied Duke for the regular-season title, and even though Duke won the ACC Tournament, the Terrapins were sent to the East Regional—perhaps because it was being played in Syracuse and not the Meadowlands or Philadelphia, Duke's homes away from home.

The Blue Devils met Indiana in the round of 16. The game didn't have nearly the hype it once had since Bob Knight had been fired at Indiana two years earlier. Indiana president Myles Brand had given Knight a "no tolerance" edict after video of him choking former Indiana player Neil Reed had become public. Knight had emphatically denied the incident before the video emerged.

After the "no tolerance" edict, Knight did an interview on ESPN with his longtime friend Digger Phelps in which he said he would have no problem at all dealing with the strict scrutiny he was under. Four months later, on September 7, Knight was in Assembly Hall when he encountered Kent Harvey, an Indiana student who was in the building picking up tickets for that Saturday's football game.

To this day, exactly what happened between the two is disputed. Harvey *did* say, "Hey Knight, what's up?" He told the *Indiana Daily Student* later that he meant to say "Mr. Knight," but the "Mr." didn't come out.

Knight reacted angrily, saying to Harvey, "It's Mr. Knight or Coach Knight to you—*not* Knight."

That was Knight's version. Harvey's version—and reports from other witnesses—maintained that Knight had grabbed Harvey's arm and used several profanities during the brief exchange.

Regardless of the specifics, Brand fired Knight three days later. He was further angered by the fact that when he'd asked Knight to cancel a weekend fishing trip to come and meet with him, Knight refused. Brand had simply had enough.

For his decision, Brand was hanged in effigy by some Indiana students. Coaches across the country—including Krzyzewski—defended Knight. Krzyzewski called the firing "tragic," which was a little over the top, and Roy Williams said if Knight had been given 100 chances to fix his behavior and failed, he should be given 100 more chances.

The firing stood. Assistant coach Mike Davis was named the new head coach, and he was in charge of the fifth-seeded team that Duke faced in the round of 16 two seasons later.

For a while, it looked like Duke would roll to a routine victory and meet upstart Kent State in the regional finals. It was 42–29 at halftime, and Duke led by 15 early in the second half. But then, slowly, things began to unravel. No one could hit a shot; Dunleavy was 5-of-16 and Williams 6-of-19. Meanwhile, Indiana star Jared Jeffries warmed up and began hitting every shot he looked at from anywhere on the court.

The lead dwindled until Indiana finally led 73–69 with under 20 seconds to play. It looked as if the game was over, but Williams hit a three *and* got fouled with three seconds on the clock. Why an Indiana player came anywhere near him at that point is inexplicable, but, after a time-out, Williams went to the line with a chance to tie the game.

Williams was never a great foul shooter—67 percent for that season and for his career—and hadn't been to the line that night.

"I was very confident I was going to make it, and we were going to play overtime," he said. "But I knew when the ball came off my hand, I'd missed. It just didn't feel right."

Remarkably, Boozer had somehow gotten position inside and grabbed the rebound. For an instant it looked as if Duke was going to *win* in regulation. But Boozer's layup fell off the rim at the buzzer and Indiana had survived 74–73.

"When Booz got the rebound, I remember thinking for an instant, 'Oh my god, we're going to win!'" Williams said. "One second later, I realized my career was over. Just like that."

It was a stunning upset. Indiana had been 22–10 coming into the game and Duke 31–3. The game reminded many Duke people of the 1998 Kentucky game, when the Blue Devils had a 17-point second-half lead and appeared to be on cruise control, and then, in what felt like the blink of an eye, the lead, the game, and the season were all gone.

"That one was tough to take because of all the circumstances," Dunleavy said. "We thought we were the best team, and we thought we were going back to the Final Four. And then, suddenly, we weren't."

The three junior stars—Williams, Boozer, and Dunleavy—had all returned to Duke to try to go back-to-back the way Laettner, Hurley, Davis, and Hill had done ten years earlier. When that dream died, they all turned pro. They were drafted second (Williams), third (Dunleavy), and 35th (Boozer). Teams shied away from Boozer in the first round because he was a 6-foot-8 inside player, and they thought he might struggle offensively in the NBA. He ended up playing in the league for thirteen years, averaged 14.6 points and 9.5 rebounds per game, and was an All-Star.

Dunleavy's father had played in the NBA for nine years and coached four different NBA teams for seventeen years. The younger Dunleavy played for fifteen seasons, averaging 11.8 points per game, and then decided to become a scout rather than a coach. In the summer of 2023, he became the general manager of the Golden State Warriors.

Williams's NBA career ended abruptly after one season. He had a solid rookie season, starting fifty-four games and averaging 9.5 points and 4.7 assists per game. But on the night of June 19, 2003, his life changed forever when he crashed a motorcycle into a streetlight in Chicago. He was going too fast, wasn't wearing a helmet, and violated his Bulls contract simply by being on the motorcycle.

Williams fractured his pelvis, severed a main nerve in his leg, and tore three ligaments in his knee—including the anterior cruciate ligament (ACL). He was lucky to live, much less ever play basketball again.

One of the first people Williams remembered seeing in the hospital was Krzyzewski, who flew to Chicago as soon as he heard about the accident. "He gave me his mother's Rosary that day," Williams said. "He said, 'You can give it back to me when you play again.' I still have it to this day."

Technically, Williams did play again, but his comeback was brief. In 2006, the New Jersey Nets signed him in preseason, but he lasted just three weeks before being cut. He then signed with the Austin Toros of what is now the NBA's G League but played in only three games before he was hurt again and decided to retire.

Williams had been through some difficult times during his lengthy recovery from his injuries, including becoming addicted to painkillers for a while. Today, he's married—to an Indiana graduate—and they have three kids. He's had a very good run working for ESPN on both television and radio, surviving the network's purge of big names in the summer of 2023. There wasn't much doubt he would find a soft landing somewhere in the not-too-distant future.

With three key players lost to the NBA, Krzyzewski was faced with what amounted to a rebuild for the 2002–3 season. *Rebuild* is a relative word. Chris Duhon, Dahntay Jones, and Daniel Ewing returned, and three talented freshmen joined them: J. J. Redick, Shelden Williams, and Shavlik Randolph.

The Blue Devils were young—but very good. They sailed through their preconference campaign 10–0 and had wins over UCLA, Michigan, Ohio State, and Georgetown. They started conference play with wins over Virginia and Wake Forest before losing on the road to Maryland, which had won the 2002 national title—helped, no doubt, by Duke going down early. In fact, the Terrapins beat Indiana—the team that had beaten Duke—in the championship game.

Neither Maryland nor Duke was as good as it had been the previous year, but both were still very solid. Duke also won a nonconference game against Butler. Afterward, in trying to compliment Butler, Krzyzewski said: "This is the kind of team we could meet in the second round of the NCAA Tournament."

Duke never did play Butler in the second round of the tournament, but the two schools both reached the round of 16 in 2003 and met a few years later in the tournament, well beyond the second round.

The Blue Devils finished the regular season 21–6 after losing the finale in Chapel Hill to an improved North Carolina team. That meant they finished the regular season 11–5 in conference play and tied for second with Maryland, two games behind Wake Forest.

Duke managed to win its fifth straight ACC Tournament, coming from 15 points behind against NC State in the final to win the title. That earned them a No. 3 seed in the West Regional—the first time they hadn't been a No. 1 or No. 2 seed since 1997.

They rolled to the Sweet Sixteen in Anaheim but lost 79–75 to a very good Kansas team there. The Jayhawks would go on to lose the national championship game to Syracuse in what turned out to be Roy Williams's last game as the coach at Kansas.

Duke appeared to be loaded for 2003–4, with Duhon, Ewing, Redick, Williams, and Randolph returning and hypertalented freshman Luol Deng joining the group. The team would win thirty-one games and make the Final Four that year.

It would also be one of the most heartbreaking seasons that Krzyzewski ever endured.

7

....

BANNER FOUR:
REALITY *and* REDEMPTION

Duke had only one senior, Chris Duhon, who would play any minutes at all in 2003–4, but the rest of the team was as talented as it was young.

J. J. Redick, whose range from outside awed people, was coming into his own as a star and led the team in scoring at just under 16 points per game. Luol Deng was right behind him and reminded people of Grant Hill—6-foot-8 and as able to play on the perimeter as on the inside. Daniel Ewing was a junior who could play either guard position, although Duhon dominated the minutes at the point. Shelden Williams and Shavlik Randolph were both athletic big men—Williams a gifted low-post scorer and Randolph blessed with a soft touch from outside.

Not surprisingly, the Blue Devils blasted through nonconference play, losing only to Purdue in November in the Great Alaska Shootout. They then started conference play at 10–0, including an overtime win at North Carolina, before losing back-to-back road games to North Carolina State and Wake Forest. They finished 13–3 in ACC play and won the regular season by two games. They went into the ACC Tournament 25–4 and easily made the final—giving them 17 straight ACC Tournament victories— where they met sixth-seeded Maryland.

The season had been a struggle for the Terrapins. They had finished 7–9 in conference play, including two losses to Duke. But they had upset Wake Forest and NC State in the first two rounds of the tournament, meaning they had wrapped up an NCAA Tournament bid, much the way NC State had done by winning its first two tournament games in 1983.

Things seemed to be going as expected, with Duke leading by 12 and the game clock under five minutes. But Maryland guard John Gilchrist, who scored 26 points and would be voted the tournament MVP, took over the game in the final few minutes. His three-point play with 15 seconds left fouled Shelden Williams out and tied the score at 77. Without Williams and clearly stunned by their collapse, the Blue Devils were completely out-played in overtime, and Maryland won 95–87—their first ACC Tournament win since 1984.

For Maryland, beating Duke in the ACC Tournament was just about as big as winning the NCAA Tournament two years earlier—a fact that Gary Williams admitted years later.

"They were just so hard to beat, and we'd been so close in the past," he said. "Coming from behind to win in the tournament final was a very big deal."

The only thorn in the day for Williams was having to accept the trophy from his boss/nemesis Debbie Yow. The two couldn't stand one another, and as luck would have it, Yow was the designated ACC athletic director that year to present the trophy.

Assistant coach Jimmy Patsos remembered the scene vividly. "Gary was as happy as I'd ever seen him," he said. "Then he saw Debbie walking on court to present the trophy, and his whole mood changed. He said to me, 'Why the hell isn't she at spring football practice or something?'"

For Duke, the loss was disappointing even though it had won the previous five ACC Tournaments. To lose the way it lost, blowing a big lead late, made it painful. Even with the loss, the Blue Devils were a No. 1 seed—sent to what was called the "Atlanta Regional," the NCAA having decided for some reason to label their regionals by city rather than region of the country.

Duke's one close game en route to the Final Four in San Antonio was in the regional final against No. 7 seed Xavier, which played them almost to the buzzer before Duke won 66–63. It was Krzyzewski's tenth trip to the Final Four, meaning he trailed only John Wooden (twelve) and Dean Smith (eleven).

Oklahoma State had won the so-called East Rutherford Regional by upsetting top-seeded St. Joseph's in the regional final, and Georgia Tech had beaten Kansas to win the St. Louis Regional. Connecticut had easily won the Phoenix Regional, winning its four games by a total of 70 points with no margin under 16 points.

All of which set up yet another epic Duke-Connecticut matchup, this one in the second game on Saturday, after a Will Bynum driving layup at the buzzer had given Georgia Tech a 67–65 victory over Oklahoma State in the opener.

The game was chippy and intense from the start. Connecticut coach Jim Calhoun was all over the officials when his star center, Emeka Okafor, picked up two quick fouls. "I guess Duke doesn't foul," he kept repeating. "We foul, but not Duke."

Okafor was called for one foul the rest of the way, while both Duke centers, Shelden Williams and Shavlik Randolph, fouled out. Apparently, Duke *did* foul.

Duke had a 75–67 lead when Williams fouled out with 3:04 to play. At that point, Krzyzewski made one of his rare coaching mistakes. He sent in Nick Horvath, his third-string center who rarely played in crucial moments, for Williams. Hindsight being 20-20 (although I said it on press row at the time), he should have put Deng on Okafor. At 6-8, Deng was big and athletic enough to guard Okafor, or to at least have a *chance* to guard Okafor.

Horvath had no chance. Okafor, who scored all 18 of his points in the second half, had seven points and three rebounds during a stunning 12–0

UConn run in the final minutes that decided the game. The Huskies led 76–75 with just under 15 seconds left when Redick drove to the basket and appeared to get hammered as he went up for the shot. There was no call, and Rashad Anderson grabbed the rebound and made two free throws for a 78–75 UConn lead. The Huskies would hold on for the 79–78 win.

The loss was much tougher for Krzyzewski to take than the Maryland loss in the ACC Tournament, when his team had also blown a big lead. As always, he was gracious in the press conference, giving credit to the Huskies and, especially, Okafor.

Underneath, he was seething.

When I approached Krzyzewski in the hallway after he'd left the media room, his opening comment was, "We got screwed."

Krzyzewski rarely blamed anyone other than himself for a loss, but he felt differently about this one. He was convinced that Calhoun's carping had affected the way the officials called the game in the second half. He was also convinced that Redick—a 90 percent free-throw shooter—should have been at the line in the game's closing seconds.

"They bought into the 'Duke gets all the calls' crap," he said. "I understand what Jim was doing, but officials working a Final Four game should be better than that."

Two nights later, Connecticut easily beat Georgia Tech in the championship game—a game that Krzyzewski and his team were convinced they should have been playing. He also believed his team would have beaten Tech and won the title.

. . . .

Unfortunately, the offseason, which began on Saturday rather than on Monday, didn't go any better.

Krzyzewski had been convinced that Deng would stay at Duke for at least three years. His parents were both educators, and he was the kind of kid who thrived in college. But when NBA scouts and agents began telling the family that Deng would probably be a lottery pick, he (and they) were swayed, and he declared for the NBA Draft. It turned out that in this case, the scouts and agents were telling the truth: he was the seventh player selected in the first round and went on to play in the league for sixteen years, averaging 14.8 points and 6.4 rebounds per season.

Duke did have two stud freshmen scheduled to arrive in the fall of 2004. One was Shaun Livingston, a 6-7 point guard from Peoria, Illinois, who was likely to take over the point from Chris Duhon. But Livingston was also being wooed by the NBA, and he, too, declared for the draft. He was the No. 4 pick in the first round and played parts of fifteen seasons, often missing major stretches because of injuries.

And then there was Kris Humphries, a 6-10 center from Minneapolis. Humphries wanted to play one year of college basketball to improve his draft status. He had little interest in academics, which is why he balked when Krzyzewski told him he had to go to summer school. Krzyzewski always required his freshmen to take summer-school classes so they would start the fall ahead of the curve academically.

Humphries refused. Instead, he enrolled at Minnesota, where he stayed for one year and was the No. 14 pick in the 2006 NBA Draft. He was an oft-injured journeyman NBA player for fifteen seasons who ultimately became best known for marrying Kim Kardashian.

The decisions made by Deng, Livingston, and Humphries caught Krzyzewski off guard. They also came at a time when he was being offered a massive contract—$40 million for five years—to coach the Los Angeles Lakers. He wasn't nearly as tempted this time as he had been by offers in the past, in spite of what had happened in the spring with player defections. However, for two reasons, he did let word get out that the Lakers had put the offer on the table: first, so the media would talk about what a loss college basketball would suffer if he left; and second, to make sure the new president at Duke, Richard H. Brodhead, understood how important Krzyzewski was to the school.

Krzyzewski *did* call his ex-boss Tom Butters to ask him what he thought about the Lakers offer. "I think if you take it, you should send me a 10 percent finder's fee," Butters said.

"Fine, if I take it, I'll send you $4,000," Krzyzewski said, referencing his first-year Duke salary of $40,000.

In the end, there was no finder's fee because he turned the Lakers down, leading to a press conference in which Brodhead more or less compared Krzyzewski to Mother Teresa, Winston Churchill, and John F. Kennedy—all of whom ranked just below the coach in the history of the world.

Krzyzewski had made his point. But he was still unhappy about what had happened to his roster.

"I'm done recruiting anyone who isn't staying at least three years," he told me that summer. "If a kid says, 'I may turn pro in a year,' or even in two years, I'm going to wish him luck and move on to someone else. I can't do this anymore. I need to coach kids for more than one year, and I need some stability for my team."

It was a noble and understandable thought. But college basketball was changing. A year later, the NBA passed what became known as the "one-and-done" rule, meaning that players had to play one year of college before being draft eligible. In the past, truly great high school players like LeBron James, Kevin Garnett, and Kobe Bryant had gone straight to the NBA out of high school. Now, the top talents had to play somewhere for at least a year.

In the 2005 NCAA Tournament, Roy Williams–coached North Carolina won the national title with a veteran team that also benefited greatly from the contributions of 6-9, 230-pound freshman Marvin Williams, who averaged 11.6 and 6.7 rebounds a game. He then turned pro and was the No. 2 pick in the NBA Draft.

Duke continued to be competitive, even without purposely recruiting one-and-dones. In fact, Krzyzewski might have done one of his best coaching jobs in 2004–5 after losing the three underclassmen he had expected to have.

Duke finished third in the ACC regular season but won the ACC Tournament for the sixth time in seven years and cruised through the first two rounds of the NCAA Tournament, led by juniors J. J. Redick and Shelden Williams. But the Blue Devils were beaten soundly, 78–68, by Michigan State in the Sweet Sixteen and finished 27–6. A good season by most standards, but not that good for Duke.

A year later, after Redick and Williams both decided to come back for their senior seasons, Duke appeared to have a possible Final Four team again. Two highly touted recruits, point guard Greg Paulus and center Josh McRoberts, had joined the team. McRoberts was one of two star big men who came out of Indiana that spring. The other was Tyler Hansbrough. They were rated about the same coming out of high school. Hansbrough became one of the best players in ACC history. McRoberts, who left Duke after two years, did not.

The Blue Devils of 2005–6 were 27–1 and had wrapped up the ACC regular-season title before they stumbled twice in the final week of the season, losing at Florida State and then losing to North Carolina on Senior Night in Cameron. They rebounded to win another ACC Tournament and still went into the NCAA Tournament as a No. 1 seed, but they didn't seem to have the bounce they'd had through most of the regular season.

They were sent to the Atlanta Regional, where they won their first two games and faced LSU in the round of 16. The Tigers were seeded fourth but had more talent than most people understood. Three of their starters—Glenn "Big Baby" Davis, Tyrus Thomas, and Garrett Temple would go on to lengthy NBA careers. As of 2023, Temple was still active, playing for his *eleventh* team.

Perhaps the Blue Devils didn't respect LSU enough, or perhaps it was just one of those nights. Shelden Williams played superbly in what was his last college game with 23 points and 13 rebounds. But he was the only player who had a good night. J. J. Redick ended his stellar college career with one of his worst shooting nights—3-of-18 from the field, including an astonishing 0-of-9 from *inside* the three-point line. The bench contributed a grand total of four points, all from DeMarcus Nelson, and LSU won going away, 62–54.

The Tigers went on to beat Texas in overtime to reach the Final Four and then put on one of the weakest Final Four performances ever seen, losing 59–45 to UCLA in the semifinals. The Bruins then went down meekly, 73–57, to Florida in the championship game.

All of which only made the LSU loss more frustrating for Duke. On most nights, the Blue Devils would have beaten the Tigers. But the NCAA Tournament isn't about "most nights"—it's about the night you actually play the game. For the second time in three seasons, a Duke team good enough to win the national championship had come up short. At least in 2004, the loss had been to the eventual champion.

Krzyzewski now faced what amounted to a rebuilding year in 2006–7. Redick and Williams graduated, as did guard Sean Dockery. The three had combined to average 52.7 points in 2006—Redick, 26.8; Williams, 18.8; and Dockery, 7.1. The rest of the team averaged 32.7, meaning that the three players who had accounted for more than 60 percent of the scoring were gone.

Another stellar freshman class was arriving, led by shooting guard Jon Scheyer, forwards Lance Thomas and Gerald Henderson, and 7-foot-1 center Brian Zoubek. Nelson, Paulus, and McRoberts were the leading returning scorers, none of them comparable in ability to Williams and Redick.

Predictably, Duke was an up-and-down team all season. Their 13–1 nonconference record was deceiving: they played eleven games in Cameron and three games at neutral sites. Their most impressive win was over 22nd-ranked Gonzaga in Madison Square Garden.

They then began ACC play with a thud, losing at home to Virginia Tech in overtime. The rest of the regular season was rocky. They lost twice to both North Carolina and Maryland and finished with an 8–8 conference mark, their worst league record since 1996, the year of Krzyzewski's return after his back issues.

Duke was the seventh seed in the ACC Tournament and lost to NC State in overtime in the first round to finish the regular season at 22–10, their first season of double-digit losses since 1996. They were given a sixth seed and sent to the West Regional (the NCAA had returned to naming regions by, you know, *regions*), which was scheduled for San Jose, California.

Because of so-called pod play, which tried to keep teams closer to home the first weekend, they were sent to Buffalo to play a very underseeded Virginia Commonwealth (VCU) team that was led by All-American Eric Maynor.

The Rams saw the game as a golden opportunity, especially against a not-great Duke team that was pretty much out of gas. Maynor hit a jumper just before the final buzzer, and VCU—actually the better team that day—won 79–77. It was yet another reminder of 1996, but this time the first-round loss was close.

The Blue Devils were better the following season. The freshmen all had a season under their belts, although Zoubek was hampered by injuries that limited his playing time. Nelson was the only senior on the team, and he averaged 14.5 points per game to lead five players who averaged double figures. Three talented freshmen contributed from day one: Kyle Singler, Nolan Smith, and Taylor King.

The team's only loss in its first twenty-three games was in overtime to Pittsburgh in Madison Square Garden. Duke was 22–1 when it hit the skids, losing back-to-back road games to Wake Forest and Miami. Then the Blue Devils ended the regular season by losing at home to North

Carolina—their third straight home loss to the Tar Heels, this time after beating them in the Dean Dome. A year later, Carolina would win in Cameron for the fourth straight year, meaning that Tyler Hansbrough finished his career with a 4–0 record in Cameron.

Carolina's season-ending win gave the Tar Heels the regular-season title and made Duke the No. 2 seed in the ACC Tournament. The Blue Devils' semifinal loss to Clemson meant they didn't get a shot to avenge the Carolina loss in the tournament final, and they were sent to the NCAA Tournament as a No. 2 seed in the West Regional.

Duke's first- and second-round games were in downtown Washington, D.C. The Blue Devils never made it to Phoenix for the regionals. In fact, they were lucky to win one game. Krzyzewski was running a high fever on the day of his team's first-round game against Belmont, and team doctor Dean Taylor wanted him to stay in bed so he might get better in time for a second-round game. Krzyzewski was adamant that he had to be at the Belmont game.

Krzyzewski knew how good Belmont was. The Bruins were one of those so-called mid-majors that were always dangerous and almost always underseeded by the tournament-committee mavens, who undoubtedly thought Belmont was just a famous horse race. The Bruins had good players and, in Rick Byrd, a superb coach. Krzyzewski knew his team needed him.

He and Taylor finally compromised: he could be on the bench during the game, but he was not to get *off* the bench. With his team down eight and under 10 minutes to go, Krzyzewski decided he'd had enough.

"Honestly, I just said, 'F— it,' if we're going to lose we're going to lose with me coaching my team," he said later.

The Blue Devils rallied and pulled out a 71–70 win.

But that was as far as they went. Two days later, they lost 73–67 to a very good West Virginia team, building a big first half lead before collapsing in the second half. Joe Mazzulla, now the coach of the Boston Celtics, came off the bench to score 13 points and lead West Virginia's rally. The Mountaineers outscored the Blue Devils, 44–33 in the second half. The loss meant Duke finished 29–9 and failed to reach the Sweet Sixteen for a second straight season.

Meanwhile, North Carolina, having won the national championship in 2005, reached the 2008 Final Four before losing to Kansas in the semifinals. The Tar Heels had again become the dominant program in the ACC.

The good news for Duke was that the freshmen who had entered in 2006 were now all going to be juniors, and Kyle Singler and Nolan Smith would be sophomores with star potential. Miles Plumlee, the oldest of three Plumlee brothers who would play for Duke (all at least 6-foot-10) joined the team as a freshman, while Taylor King, unhappy with his playing time, transferred to Villanova.

The 2008–9 season was similar to the previous season. The Blue Devils were very good—they finished with a record of 30–7—but not as good as they had been in the past. They were swept by North Carolina in the regular season, but they did win the ACC Tournament in the Georgia Dome, beating Florida State in the championship game. It was their eighth tournament title since 1999 and Krzyzewski's eleventh overall. So much for Al Featherston's statement about the ACC tournament being Krzyzewski's Achilles' heel.

The NCAA Tournament that year was another story.

Duke was the No. 2 seed in the East Regional and played its first- and second-round games in Greensboro. The Blue Devils easily beat Binghamton in the first round and then held off Texas 74–69 in the second round to reach the Sweet Sixteen for the first time since 2006.

From there, they went to Boston and were routed 77–54 by third-seeded Villanova. The game wasn't really that close. The Wildcats broke it open early in the second half and outscored the Blue Devils 51–31 in the final 20 minutes. It was Duke's worst NCAA Tournament loss since the UNLV championship game in 1990.

Villanova went on to make the Final Four, where it was soundly beaten by North Carolina. The Tar Heels went on to crush Michigan State two nights later on a snowy night in Detroit to win the national title. It was Carolina's second national championship in five years, and the banners being raised in the Dean Dome did not go unnoticed ten miles up the road in Durham.

....

"In an ideal world, there would be no such thing as one-and-done. I think my strength as a coach has always been communicating with my players and getting them to understand how they can get better from year to year. It's what I've always enjoyed most about coaching. But there comes a time when you look around and realize that a lot of great players are either going to play *for* you or *against* you. In the end, I decided I wanted them playing for me."

Mike Krzyzewski was talking about the most difficult decision of his coaching career. Back in the summer of 2004, he had vowed not to recruit players unless he believed they were going to stay at Duke for at least three years. He had stuck to that vow after the one-and-done rule became part of college basketball in 2006.

Duke had continued to produce very good teams year in and year out. From 2005 through 2009, Duke was 139–34, meaning the Blue Devils' average record was just below 28–7. They made the NCAA Tournament all five years and won the ACC Tournament three times. They reached the Sweet Sixteen of the NCAAs three times during that stretch.

That record would be considered superb by normal standards. The problem was that the standards Krzyzewski and most Duke people expected the team to live up to weren't normal. Duke had been to seven Final Fours in nine years in one stretch, and then, after a five-year drought, had gotten there three more times in six seasons. There had also been the three national championships. That was the level of success Krzyzewski and Duke measured themselves against.

Another issue was that Duke's archrivals down the street in Chapel Hill were on a remarkable run. During those same five seasons, the Tar Heels were 157–26. They won two ACC titles, but far more important, they were dominant in NCAA Tournament play. They won two national titles and went to three Final Fours. They failed to make the Elite Eight once—in 2006, when they were upset in the second round by George Mason's miracle team. Their head-to-head record against Duke was 7–3.

"What happened my freshman year was a shock to us all," Jon Scheyer said. "That sort of record [22–11] isn't what we expected when we came to Duke. We all knew the history, and we all knew the kind of success that was expected. We expected it, too. Except it didn't happen."

Brian Zoubek, also a part of that class, felt the same way. "Duke was Duke, and that didn't mean losing in the first round of the ACC Tournament or the NCAA Tournament. For us, and I know for Coach K, that season and the next couple were a struggle. We all felt it, and, yeah, Carolina being so good certainly made it tougher."

Zoubek was injured during his sophomore season during a late-night pickup game in Cameron with Scheyer.

"I still give Jon a hard time about that," Zoubek said, laughing. "I was on a date, and he called me and said the guys were getting together to play some pickup. I went, and he was the only one there. So we played one-on-one for a while. I went up for a rebound and came down on his shoe."

Zoubek had fractured the fifth metatarsal in his foot. Two days later, he had surgery to have a screw inserted into the foot. He had a second surgery several months later, and the foot never felt completely healed, especially during his junior year. "It felt as if every time I was about to be healthy, something happened to set me back," he said. "To call it frustrating would be a vast understatement."

Late in the 2008–9 season, Krzyzewski decided to move Scheyer to point guard for two reasons. First, senior Greg Paulus was struggling, and Krzyzewski thought Scheyer's ability to score while playing the position would help the team. And second, sophomore Nolan Smith was playing too well not to get more minutes at the shooting-guard spot.

Smith was the son of Derek Smith, who had played on Louisville's national championship team in 1980. He then played and coached in the NBA until his death from cancer in 1996, when his son was eight.

"He was my inspiration to play basketball," Nolan said. "I was around the game from the time I was little, and I knew how good he had been. I aspired to grow up to be like him as a player and a person."

He was a star throughout high school. He went to two different schools in the Washington, D.C., area and then enrolled at Oak Hill Academy in Virginia—a prep-school basketball powerhouse. Oak Hill was 80–2 his two seasons there, and almost everyone assumed Smith would follow his father to Louisville.

"First time I saw I was going to Louisville was seventh grade," he said, laughing. "But I wasn't sure if I wanted to follow in my dad's footsteps, always have the 'Derek Smith's son' pressure on me. The key was Johnny Dawkins, who had been a teammate of my dad's in Philadelphia. He was 'Uncle Johnny' to me growing up. He and my mom were talking one night when I was a junior, and he said, 'I assume Nolan's going to Louisville.' She said that wasn't necessarily true. The next day, Coach K called. My mom and I both fell in love with him and with Duke."

Moving Scheyer to the point not only made Smith a starter; it also made Duke a better team offensively.

"I think that turned out to be a key decision," Scheyer said. "I had been a backup point guard my first two years, so it wasn't like he was asking me to do something I hadn't done in the past. Plus, I think with Nolan and me at the guards and Kyle [Singler] playing small forward, we were a dangerous team outside."

....

Duke lost one key player from the 2008–9 team: co-leading scorer (with Singler) Gerald Henderson, who had averaged 16.5 points per game and decided to pass up his senior season to turn pro. He was the 12th player taken in that summer's NBA Draft and ended up playing in the NBA for thirteen seasons.

Duke returned Scheyer and Smith at the guard spots, Singler and Lance Thomas at forward, and question marks at center. Miles and Mason Plumlee were both there, and so was freshman Ryan Kelly, who was more a forward than a center.

And then there was Zoubek. He began the 2009–10 season still trying to get healthy and earn playing time. "I wanted to play, but I also wanted my teammates to trust me when I played," he said. "I wanted to be in the game at the end, with the game on the line, and to make plays when I was needed. Finally, in early February, it began to happen."

Zoubek was in a tight game late at Boston College and played well at North Carolina, a game Duke won easily. The Tar Heels had finally come back to earth that winter, and they landed with a thud, finishing with a 5–11 ACC record—tied for ninth—and a 20–17 record for the season. They failed to make the NCAA Tournament and had to settle for the (embarrassing for them) NIT.

Things were so bad that, after a first-round ACC Tournament loss to Georgia Tech, Roy Williams stood in a hallway in the Greensboro Coliseum talking to me when he saw Carolina athletic director Dick Baddour coming in his direction.

"I better go talk to my boss," Williams said. "See if he wants to make a change."

He was kidding... sort of.

Maryland came to Cameron after the Carolina game tied with Duke for first place in the ACC. Krzyzewski gave Zoubek his first start, and he responded with 16 points and 17 rebounds in 22 minutes in a 77–56 Duke rout.

"It was the feeling I'd waited to have for four years," he said. "It was great."

It also made Duke a different team. Zoubek allowed the other four players to be more aggressive on defense because they knew they had a 7-1 shot blocker behind them. Plus, he became a rebounding force on both ends of the floor. In that first start against Maryland, eight of his 17 rebounds were on the offensive end.

"He and [Kentucky's] DeMarcus Cousins were the two best rebounders in the country," Scheyer said. "If I had to choose, I'd take Zoubs. He was that good."

In ten of the fourteen games he started, Zoubek had at least 10 rebounds, and he had nine in one other game. Cousins went on to be the No. 5 pick in the NBA Draft. But he never played in a Final Four like Zoubek did.

"We don't win the championship without Zoubs," Smith said. "It's that simple."

With Zoubek joining fellow seniors Thomas and Scheyer and juniors Smith and Singler in the starting lineup, Duke had one of the oldest teams in the country.

Ironically, Krzyzewski had finally given up his anti-one-and-done stance that fall when he signed Kyrie Irving, who everyone in the country knew was going to be a one-and-done. But the winter and spring of 2010 belonged to the old guys. After Zoubek became a starter, the Blue Devils lost only once more, at Maryland, on Senior Night for Terrapins star Greivis Vásquez. It was a court-storming night for Maryland, and the win allowed the Terrapins to tie Duke for the ACC title, both teams posting 13–3 records.

In spite of the team's record, there was tension between the players and the coaching staff throughout Duke's regular season.

"We were pissed at the way we lost to Villanova in 2009," Scheyer said. "We had a chip on our shoulders that whole season. We knew we'd gotten better with each season, but we still weren't good enough. We had one last chance. The coaches kept telling us that we were a good team, but not a great team or even a very good team. That bothered us because we knew we were giving everything we had. Looking back now, I understand it, but back then it bothered us."

Nolan Smith, who was a junior, confirmed the tension. "We had the kind of team where we knew what Coach K wanted almost all the time," he said. "We were winning a lot of games, but nothing seemed to be quite good enough [for the coaches]. I think after that Maryland game, we kind of looked at one another and said, 'Okay, enough is enough. We aren't losing again.'"

Maryland was upset in the first round of the ACC Tournament, while Duke went on to win it—making it nine tournament titles in twelve years. The Blue Devils were sent to the South Regional as a No. 1 seed. Maryland was sent to the Midwest Regional as a No. 4 seed, playing its first two games in Spokane, Washington—the site of Krzyzewski's first NCAA Tournament game in 1984.

And like that long-ago Duke team, Maryland failed to advance to the Sweet Sixteen, losing in heartbreaking fashion to Michigan State. The Spartans dominated for most of the game but lost their leading scorer, Kalin Lucas, late in the first half to what turned out to be a torn ACL. They led by as many as 16 points in the second half and still led by 10 with a little more than six minutes left.

But Vásquez rallied his team. He scored nine points in the last three minutes, including a driving floater with 6.6 seconds left that gave the Terrapins an 83–82 lead. Michigan State didn't call a time-out, and Draymond Green pushed the ball upcourt. He dribbled left and stopped at the top of the key, looking for someone open. He appeared to try to slide a pass to Delvon Roe, a 6-8 forward who was an inside scorer. But Roe *ducked under* the pass, and it went right to Korie Lucious, who was playing in Lucas's place. Lucious caught the pass, took one dribble, and went up to shoot a three, releasing the ball just before the buzzer. It swished, and Michigan State escaped with an 85–83 victory.

That night, I called Gary Williams to offer condolences. "I'm too old to ever get over that one," Williams said.

As it turned out, that was his last NCAA Tournament game as Maryland's coach.

. . . .

Duke was sent to Jacksonville, Florida, for the first two rounds of the NCAAs and cruised through those games to get to Houston. The regional there was more difficult. Purdue hung close for most of Friday night before Duke prevailed 70–57. The regional final was against Baylor, whose campus was 160 miles from Houston.

"At that point, I don't think playing a road game bothered us," Smith said. "We'd played plenty of them already."

The game was close until the final three minutes, when Scheyer hit two crucial threes and Duke pulled away to win 78–71.

Duke advanced to the Final Four in Indianapolis—Krzyzewski's eleventh, tying him with Dean Smith, and Duke's first since the UConn collapse in 2004. They would play West Virginia after the Mountaineers had stunned Kentucky in the East Regional final. The Wildcats missed their first 21 three-point shots and ended up 4-of-32 in the game as West Virginia hung on to win 73–66.

That game in Syracuse turned out to be WVU's zenith for the tournament. Against Duke, the Mountaineers trailed from the start. The Blue Devils built a 39–31 margin at halftime and then dominated the second half en route to a 78–57 win. Scheyer scored 23 points; Singler, 21; and Smith, 19.

That set up the championship game against Butler, the team Krzyzewski had once talked about as a possible second-round opponent. The Bulldogs had come a long way from those days. They had gone into the tournament clearly underseeded as a No. 5 and had beaten top-seeded Syracuse and second-seeded Kansas State to win the West Regional. They then took care of Michigan State 52–50 in the first game of the Final Four.

Butler had a soon-to-be first-round draft pick in 6-foot-9 Gordon Hayward, who had grown up in Brownsburg, Indiana, fourteen miles from Lucas Oil Stadium. The Butler campus and its historic Hinkle Fieldhouse were only 6.4 miles across town. It was in Hinkle that the famous "Milan Miracle," the basis for the film *Hoosiers*, took place in 1954. Bobby Plump, the real-life Jimmy Chitwood, was a Butler graduate and owned a bar in Indianapolis called Plump's Last Shot. Most of the national media made its way there to hear Plump retell the story of his last-second jump shot that gave Milan its improbable 32–30 victory over Muncie Central in the state championship game.

Clearly, the Duke-Butler final was seen by many as another *Hoosiers* moment—the underdog midwestern kids whom no one had picked to get this far against the superpower that had become the heavy favorite as the tournament moved on.

It was, in short, David vs. Goliath in shorts.

"Talk about a road game," Nolan Smith said, laughing. "There were 70,000 people in the building, and all but a couple thousand were for Butler."

Smith was not exaggerating. Who doesn't root for David? Who roots for Goliath?

But Butler's success was not a fluke. In Brad Stevens, the Bulldogs had a brilliant young coach—he was thirty-three at the time but looked twenty-three—who was a star in the making. In addition to Hayward in the role of Jimmy Chitwood, they had a veteran team that played remarkable defense.

"It may have been the most exhausting 40 minutes I ever played," said Scheyer, who played 37 minutes while Smith and Singler played 40 apiece. "Every possession was physical. They were big and strong, and they put their bodies on you. We knew almost right away how tough it was going to be to win."

"Truth is, after the way we played against West Virginia, we thought somewhere we'd make an eight- or ten-point run and pull away, but we never did," Smith said. "They were too good for that."

Neither team led by more than five points the entire night. Duke led 33–32 at halftime, and the game swung back and forth the entire second half. The level of physical play was so intense that a *Washington Post* reporter lucky enough to be seated on the front row (me) could literally *hear* the contact the way you hear the collisions from the sideline during a football game.

Singler, who was voted the Most Outstanding Player of the Final Four, was heroic the entire night. He led both teams in scoring with 19 points and had nine rebounds, one less than Zoubek. But his most important work came at the defensive end, where he held Hayward to 2-of-11 shooting and 12 points. Duke's starters outplayed the Butler starters, but the Butler bench contributed 15 points in 47 minutes. Duke's bench played 17 minutes and didn't score.

Which was why Butler appeared to be the fresher team in the waning minutes. Perhaps it was the bench; perhaps it was the crowd.

"We were feeling it," Smith said about the end-of-game fatigue. "But we'd come too far not to finish the job."

Duke led 60–59 (the first team to score 60 points against Butler in the tournament) when Singler missed a jump shot and the loose ball went out-of-bounds off Zoubek's foot with 33.7 seconds to go. The shot clock (35 seconds back then) was off.

One could almost feel Hayward stepping into the Butler huddle and saying, "Coach, I'll make it."

First, though, Zoubek deflected a pass out-of-bounds with 13.6 seconds left. After a Butler time-out, Krzyzewski put Zoubek on the ball on the in-bounds pass—something he'd never done before. Butler couldn't get the ball inbounds and had to use its final time-out. That would prove critical in the final sequence.

Butler finally got the ball where it wanted it—in the hands of Hayward, who was at the top of the key (just the spot it had gone to Plump forty-six years earlier). He dribbled to his right around a high ball screen, got to the baseline, and went up to shoot.

Zoubek was inside the key, guarding Butler center Matt Howard. "I had to make a split-second decision," he said. "If I left Howard and Hayward passed him the ball, he'd be wide open for a dunk. But something told me Hayward was going to shoot, and I had to make a move at him."

Zoubek sprang toward Hayward, and Hayward, seeing the 7-1 Zoubek coming at him from seemingly out of nowhere, had to lean back a little to get the shot over Zoubek's hand. That was the difference: the ball hit the side of the rim and bounced back in the direction of Zoubek, who grabbed the rebound and was fouled instantly by Butler's Shelvin Mack.

There were 3.6 seconds left on the clock.

Stevens, with no time-outs left, could not to try to freeze Zoubek, a 55 percent foul shooter. Krzyzewski certainly wasn't going to call time. So everyone marched to the other end of the court.

"I remember thinking that I was the last person I thought would end up on the line with a national championship at stake," Zoubek said. "But I was in a bubble, just staring at the rim."

Zoubek swished the first shot. That meant if he made the second, Duke couldn't lose in regulation. It also meant that Butler would get to run an inbounds play, the kind that teams practice all the time with a short clock.

Krzyzewski jumped off the bench, waved at Zoubek, and said, "Miss it, Zoubs."

Scheyer, standing behind Zoubek, was surprised—maybe even shocked —and he thought he heard assistant coaches Chris Collins and Steve Wojciechowski saying, "Go ahead and make it."

"I tried to get Zoubs's attention, but even though he was only a few feet from me, he couldn't hear me," Scheyer said. "The noise was unbelievable."

Zoubek had heard his instruction from Krzyzewski. "I didn't know how to feel," he said. "Heck, I could have missed it without trying to miss—I was 55 percent from the line, anyway. What crossed my mind was, 'Make sure you hit the rim, because if you airball it, they get to take it out-of-bounds.'"

He hit the back rim. Hayward quickly grabbed the rebound and began racing upcourt. Since the lead was two, no one dared go near him to foul. As Hayward approached midcourt, Howard hammered Singler with what was either one of the greatest screens in basketball history or a clear foul that wasn't called because of the circumstances.

With Singler on the floor, trying to figure out what city he was in, Hayward raced across midcourt and released a shot just before the buzzer. The shot was on line all the way and looked like it might go in. It hit the backboard and side rim before bouncing away.

Lying on the floor helplessly, Singler watched the ball as it flew through the air. "Honestly, I thought it might go in," he said later.

Zoubek also wondered. "For a second, I thought, 'Is this how my career ends?'" he said. "I've honestly had nightmares about that screen the guy threw on Kyle. We'd come so far to get to that point, *I'd* come so far to get to that point. It was a terrifying second."

Scheyer, who was a few feet away from Hayward when he shot the ball, insisted he was never worried. "I turned around and watched it, and I really thought it was off," he said. "It honestly didn't cross my mind that it would go in."

Krzyzewski said he has only one memory of the moment. "My mind was a blank," he said. "It was such an intense game, the best final I'd been in up to that point [it was his eighth]. Both teams were so good, especially on defense. I just remember thinking the shot's not going in. It came close, but it didn't go in, and we celebrated."

It was Krzyzewski's fourth national championship, tying him for second place on the all-time list with Adolph Rupp—Duke's past "almost" coach. The attendance was 70,941, and it felt as if everyone in the building was drained by the finish. It got very quiet, except in the joyous Duke corner of the building when the final shot bounced away.

David's shot at Goliath had missed—barely. Mathematicians broke the shot down later and found that Hayward had been off by three inches.

"It's amazing the difference between winning and losing a game like that," Scheyer said. "You're going to carry the memory with you forever, win or lose. When you win, you're part of history, and you celebrate the win for the rest of your life. You go to reunions and laugh about everything that happened. You point out the banner to your kids. If you lose . . . well, I can't imagine."

Jay Bilas could. "Every year at the end of the national championship game, I don't watch the winners celebrate," he said. "I watch the losers, because I know exactly how they feel."

Nolan Smith wondered why a movie hasn't been made about Butler in spite of the loss. "If the shot goes in, they go into production the next day," he said. "Even though it didn't, I'm surprised no one made a movie out of it. They were loveable, we weren't. But thank goodness we won."

For Smith, it was a movie-like ending. Thirty years earlier, his father's Louisville team had won the national title at Market Square Arena, which was a few miles from Lucas Oil Stadium. "It was cool," he said. "Very, very cool."

Naturally, Zoubek was asked in the postgame press conference how he felt when Krzyzewski ordered him to miss the free throw. Before he could answer, Krzyzewski said, "You don't play for me anymore, Zoubs, you can say anything you want."

Zoubek laughed and said, "I honestly don't know how I felt. I just did what Coach told me to do."

Thirteen years later, Zoubek's answer hadn't really changed. "Like I said then, I might have missed without trying to miss. All I know is, we won."

The best part for the players came after the nets had come down and the media had been spoken to at length. When Krzyzewski got his players alone in the locker room, he looked at them and said, "*Now*, you're a great team."

Every player remembered that. "All year long, he'd said, 'You're a good team, you're a very good team, but you're still not a great team,'" Scheyer said. "All it took for us to be a great team was to win the national championship. In the end, that was fine with us."

8

....

BANNER FIVE: EIGHT *Is* ENOUGH

Two things had happened while Duke was on its way to the national title in 2010—one important to Duke specifically, one important to all of college basketball.

The latter was the NCAA's aborted attempt to expand the basketball tournament in order to bank a few million more dollars on it. With the TV contract with CBS expiring after 2010, there was concern that the new deal might not be as lucrative as the previous one. Even television networks have budgets—sort of.

And so the NCAA floated two ideas: one for a 96-team tournament and one for going to 128 teams. At that time, the tournament consisted of 65 teams—the last team added in 2001 when the Mountain West Conference became eligible for an automatic bid. Rather than simply lose one at-large bid, the all-knowing basketball committee added a 65th team so that the big-money schools wouldn't lose a bid. The last two automatic-bid schools in the tournament were consigned to playing in Dayton, Ohio, in a "play-in" game for a 16th seed. Inevitably, one of the schools—but not both—came from one of the two all-Black conferences.

Of course, in NCAA-speak, there was no play-in game, just an "opening round" game. The round of 64 became the "second round," one of the dumbest euphemisms in history.

I was actually involved in one of the events that led, at least indirectly, to the merciful death of the 96-team idea.

Commissioner Mark Emmert annually held a Thursday press conference at the Final Four. Greg Shaheen was the NCAA's director of publicity at the time, and he was given the horrific assignment of explaining to the media why a 96-team tournament would somehow benefit the "student-athletes."

Reading from a script, Shaheen kept telling us that an extra round of games would mean fewer games the first week for many teams and, thus, less class time missed. It didn't take a math genius to figure out that teams would have to play *three* games the next week to reach the Final Four, but Shaheen wasn't going there.

I did.

"Greg, what about class time the second week?" I asked.

"Well, John, as I said, the student-athletes wouldn't have to be away as much during the first week as under the current schedule."

The guy moving the microphone around the room tried to grab the mike back from me. I held on tight.

"Greg, you've made that clear, but wouldn't teams have to play three games, basically be on the road, the entire second week?"

"We're not talking about the second week, we're talking about the first."

"Don't you need to talk about all three weeks?"

By now, there were two volunteers wrestling the mike away from me.

"I don't think you understand me," Shaheen said.

"No Greg, I think we *all* understand you," I said and finally gave up the mike.

An hour later, I got a call from Lesley Ann Wade, a CBS public-relations person. That morning, she had asked if I would come on CBS's *The Early Show* the next day, and I'd said yes.

"We don't need you anymore in the morning," she said.

I wasn't that disappointed. I've never been a huge fan of 6:00 a.m. wake-ups.

"Okay," I said. "How come?"

"After what you just did to Greg Shaheen in that press conference, there's no way we can have you on."

I had violated the CBS/NCAA rule of see no evil.

As it turned out, CBS was able to persuade the TNT network to partner with it in the new contract. The NCAA got its money (lots of it), and the tournament only expanded to 68 teams. The NCAA used the new deal as an excuse to increase the number of teams going to Dayton to eight, including four at-large teams. This gave the networks more games to sell and allowed them to call the two nights in Dayton the "First Four." As in, the first four games, completely different than the Final Four, which consisted of the last four *teams.*

The only outcome of all this that bothered me was that Emmert and his cronies used the press conference that day as part of the reason it fired Shaheen a year later. I know this because Shaheen told me that was the case when it happened.

Greg was a friend, he was good at his job, and I always got along with him. I called him out at the press conference because, well, someone had to do it. Under orders from Emmert and company, he had been perpetrating what amounted to a hoax. I had looked around the room before asking for the microphone in the hope that someone who wasn't despised by the NCAA would ask the question. No one did.

The event that was significant to Duke was the arrival of Kyrie Irving as the first unofficially/official one-and-done Krzyzewski had recruited. The other important addition going into the 2010–11 season was sophomore Seth Curry—the younger brother of Stephen—who had transferred from Liberty and had sat out the previous season.

Irving and Curry joined a team that had lost seniors Jon Scheyer, Lance Thomas, and Brian Zoubek but returned Nolan Smith and Kyle Singler, along with Andre Dawkins and the Plumlee brothers.

As usual, the Blue Devils were dominant in preconference play, going 12–0. There were, however, two important moments before the New Year.

On December 4, Duke and Butler played a made-for-TV game in the New Jersey Meadowlands. Late in the game, with Duke leading comfortably, Irving went after a loose ball and somehow tore a ligament in his right big toe. Duke won the game easily, 82–70, but Irving would miss the next twenty-six games, not returning until the first round of the NCAA Tournament.

The second big moment was far more pleasant. On December 29, playing at UNC Greensboro, Krzyzewski won his 880th game. That was one more than Dean Smith had won.

I was there that night, and as the crowd came to its feet and started to leave after Duke's 108–62 victory, I could hear Jim Valvano's voice in my head dating to a lunch at Mama Leone's in New York City thirty-four years earlier.

"Come on, go ahead and do your Dean [imitation]," Valvano said. "There's no way the three of us *combined* [Valvano, Krzyzewski, and Tom Penders] will win as many games as Dean."

For the record, when Krzyzewski retired in 2022 with 1,202 wins, he, Valvano, and Penders had combined to win 2,198 games.

The best part of the day for me had come at lunch. I had told Krzyzewski I wanted to spend time with him that day to write about the historic evening. "The bus leaves for Greensboro at 2:30," he said. "Meet me in my office. We can talk on the bus and then in the locker room before the game. That should be enough time, right?"

Plenty.

I arrived in Durham in time to go to lunch with one of my mentors, Bill Brill, who had graduated from Duke in 1952, and Mike Cragg, who had become Krzyzewski's right-hand man during his twenty-three years at the school as an administrator.

"When are you talking to Coach K?" Cragg asked.

"On the bus going to Greensboro," I said.

Cragg looked baffled. "You came all the way down here to talk to him on his cell phone?"

"No, I came down here to talk to him from the next seat."

Cragg was shaking his head vehemently. "You must have misunderstood. The only person who ever rides the bus who isn't part of the team is Mickie. *I* don't even ride that bus."

I repeated to Cragg what Krzyzewski had said. He kept shaking his head.

"I don't get it," he said. "Why would he let you ride the bus?"

I had my answer ready for that one.

"Because I was in the f—ing Denny's," I said.

....

Duke was still very good after Kyrie Irving's injury, but not the same. The Blue Devils' unbeaten skein ended at fifteen at a place where they often lost: Florida State. By then, Leonard Hamilton had built a first-class program.

They did manage to dodge their annual NC State bullet in Raleigh but then lost to the Wolfpack in Cameron. They split with North Carolina and then won another ACC Tournament. Nolan Smith had taken over as the point guard after Irving's injury, and everything in the offense started with him. He averaged 20.6 points per game, was the ACC's leading scorer, and was voted ACC player of the year and the ACC Tournament's most valuable player.

Smith would also become the only player off the 2010 championship team to be a first-round pick in the NBA Draft, going 21st that summer to the Portland Trail Blazers. Singler was drafted in the second round—the 33rd pick—by the Detroit Pistons. None of the seniors from that title team—Scheyer, Thomas, or Zoubek—were drafted, although Thomas did make the New Orleans Pelicans a year later and had a seven-year NBA career, most of it with the New York Knicks.

Their victory in the ACC Tournament made Duke a No. 1 NCAA seed again, this time in the West Regional, although their first two games, courtesy of the "pod" system, were in Charlotte. Irving returned to the lineup in an easy opening-round victory over Hampton before the Blue Devils were lucky to survive, 73–71, in a second-round game against Michigan.

Smith had 24 points in that game, including the winning basket in the closing seconds. But it was clear that the team was still trying to adjust to the presence of Irving. Even though Irving was coming off the bench, the offense wasn't flowing the way it was when everyone, including Smith, knew that Smith was running the offense.

"We probably needed one more week, two or three games, to figure out how to play with Kyrie again," Smith said. "He was out for more than three months. You learn to play a certain way during a stretch like that. Then he comes back, and you know how good he is, but nothing feels quite the same, at least not for a little while."

The Michigan game proved to be a harbinger. Four nights later, in Anaheim, the Blue Devils led Arizona 44–38 at halftime. They were blown out from there, outscored 55–33 in the second half, with the Wildcats' Derrick Williams exploding to finish with 32 points. That performance almost certainly led to Williams being the No. 2 pick in the NBA Draft, even though he went on to have a journeyman career.

Irving, playing his eleventh and final college game, had 28 points, but Smith, still not feeling comfortable, shot 3-of-14 and had only eight points in his final college performance. Irving was then taken with the No. 1 pick in the draft by Cleveland, which had just lost LeBron James following the "Decision" a year earlier.

"If Kyrie doesn't get hurt, if he plays the whole season, we win the national championship again," Smith said. "I'm 100 percent convinced of that—100 percent."

Nothing is 100 percent in the NCAA Tournament. The championship game was played between Butler—which had struggled without Gordon Hayward (who had been the 14th pick in the NBA Draft) during the regular season but made it to a second straight Final Four as a No. 8 seed—and Connecticut, which had started the bloated (sixteen-team) Big East Tournament as the No. 9 seed.

The Huskies won five games to win the Big East, went into the NCAAs as the No. 3 seed in the West, and won six more games to become national champions. They survived 56–55 in the semifinals against Kentucky, then beat Butler 53–41 in what might have been the ugliest championship game on record.

"It looked beautiful to me," UConn coach Jim Calhoun said when it was mercifully over.

Beauty, as the saying goes, is in the eye of the beholder.

. . . .

The next three seasons didn't provide a lot of joy at Duke, although there were moments.

Austin Rivers, son of Celtics coach Doc Rivers, replaced Irving as the 2011–12 team's one-and-done. Quinn Cook and Marshall Plumlee, two non-one-and-done freshmen who would be critical players in the future, also joined the team. Plumlee decided to redshirt, meaning there were only two Plumlees in uniform during the season—Miles, a senior, and Mason, a junior.

The first moment of the season belonged to Krzyzewski. The win over Michigan the previous season had been his 900th, meaning he was just two shy of Bob Knight's all-time record for college victories.

After two easy wins at home, Duke traveled to Madison Square Garden to play Michigan State in the Champions Classic, an early-season ESPN event that featured Duke, Michigan State, Kansas, and Kentucky playing each other in different combinations and venues each year.

Knight had retired from Texas Tech midway through the 2007–8 season (his seventh as coach of the Red Raiders) and had been hired almost instantly by ESPN, which badly wanted to make him a star. But Knight had no real interest in broadcasting; he thought it beneath him to go to production meetings and pregame shootarounds, or to talk to coaches about their team before a game—all important parts of the job for most people.

Knight still understood the game better than just about anyone, but he often didn't know players' names at the start of a game and clearly had done little prep work. For several years, ESPN overlooked those foibles because, well, he was Bob Knight. And there was *no* doubt that he was going to be assigned to work what might be the game in which his former pupil passed him as the all-time winningest coach.

Knight, being Knight, showed up for the game in a garish Michigan State green sweater. He had always refused to wear a jacket and tie on-air, and ESPN even went so far as to put his play-by-play man in a sweater so the contrast wouldn't be quite as noticeable. The green sweater that night was impossible not to notice.

This was during the period when Knight and Krzyzewski were cordial, so Krzyzewski's only comment at the time was, "It's just coach being coach."

Duke won a tense game 74–69, and when it was over, Krzyzewski was escorted over to the TV broadcast position for a postgame interview. When he arrived, he and Knight hugged awkwardly, and Knight, on mike, said, "Not bad for a point guard who couldn't shoot."

Not exactly gracious, but it was the best Knight could summon in the moment.

With Rivers the team's leading scorer, the Blue Devils got off to a 12–2 nonconference start. They won the Maui Invitational (for a third time) before losing at Ohio State and in the nonconference finale to Temple.

Duke and Temple played each other often because Krzyzewski and Temple coach Fran Dunphy had served in the army together and were teammates on the all-army team. They had remained friends through the years.

"Even when we were teammates, you could tell he understood basketball better than the rest of us did," said Dunphy, who had won 596 games himself going into the 2023–24 season. "If he sat next to you on the bench to make a point, you listened."

Duke started 4–0 in ACC play, then lost (at home!) to Florida State. The Blue Devils went to the Dean Dome to play North Carolina on February 8 with a 19–4 record after another home loss, this one to Miami.

The game in Chapel Hill turned out to be the highlight of the season and of Austin Rivers's one-year Duke career. Carolina led almost the entire night and by as many as 13 in the second half. They were up by 10 with two and a half minutes left. But the Tar Heels got piss-factored in the final two minutes.

After several clutch shots by Duke, Carolina's Tyler Zeller accidentally tipped a Ryan Kelly air ball into the basket to cut the margin to 83–82 with 14.2 seconds to play. Zeller then made the first of two free throws but missed the second, giving Duke one last chance. Rivers brought the ball upcourt, drifted to his right, and launched a three-point shot over the seven-foot Zeller's outstretched hand with one second on the clock. It swished as the buzzer sounded for an 85–84 Duke win, sending most of the 21,750 in the Dean Dome into silent shock.

Duke ended up finishing second in the regular season (behind Florida State) and then lost to the Seminoles in the semifinals of the ACC Tournament. As a result, the Blue Devils were sent to Greensboro as a No. 2 NCAA seed and faced Lehigh, the Patriot League champion.

The Mountain Hawks were not your typical Patriot League team for one reason: C. J. McCollum. He had been overlooked not only by the power schools coming out of high school but also by most mid-majors. He landed at Lehigh, and it was apparent early that a lot of schools had missed out.

As a freshman, McCollum averaged 19.1 points per game and led Lehigh to the Patriot League title. The first time American University coach Jeff Jones saw him play, he shook his head and said, "That is not a Patriot League talent."

Unfortunately for Jones and the rest of the league, McCollum never transferred in spite of numerous offers to do so. By 2012, his junior year, he had put on muscle and improved his outside shot. He again led Lehigh to the Patriot League championship, and the Mountain Hawks were seeded 15th, meaning they played Duke in the first round.

There's no doubt the Blue Devils overlooked Lehigh—15th seeds had won only five games in the tournament in twenty-seven years—and McCollum made them pay, scoring 30 points to go with his six assists and six rebounds. The Blue Devils shot 41 percent as a team and lost 75–70. Austin Rivers scored 19 points in his last college game but shot just 5-of-14 from the field. The better team won the game

"This is why basketball's a beautiful game," Krzyzewski said afterward. The look on his face indicated it was more shocking than beautiful.

Rivers and McCollum were both picked No. 10 in the NBA Draft—Rivers in 2012 and McCollum in 2013, after he graduated from Lehigh with a degree in journalism. Rivers has averaged 8.5 points per game in the NBA, playing for seven teams. McCollum has averaged 19.1 points per game with Portland and New Orleans and has been an All-Star twice. He is also the president of the NBA Players Association. His journalism degree no doubt helped.

Rivers was the only key player who left after the 2011–12 season, and Krzyzewski was able to recruit two highly thought-of freshmen: Rasheed Sulaimon, a 6-4 shooting guard from Houston, and Amile Jefferson, a 6-7 forward from Philadelphia. Sulaimon was an instant starter who averaged 11.6 points per game as a freshman. Jefferson backed up the inside players, notably Mason Plumlee, who blossomed as a senior and led the team in scoring, averaging 17.6 points per game. Seth Curry, also a senior, averaged 15 points per game. He wasn't the shooter his big brother Steph was, but he was very good.

It was, in most ways, a typical Duke regular season: a fast start that included wins over Kentucky, Louisville (in the final of the Battle 4 Atlantis), and Ohio State; a 15–0 record carried into January; and then losses at North Carolina State and Miami.

The Hurricanes were in their first season under Jim Larrañaga, the coach who had led George Mason to the Final Four in 2006. They went 15–3 to win the ACC's regular season title, finishing a game ahead of Duke at 14–4. The Blue Devils cost themselves the title by losing late at Maryland and at Virginia. They were then stunned in their first ACC Tournament game by seventh-seeded Maryland, the first time they hadn't at least reached the tournament semifinals since 1997.

How important was it to Maryland to beat Duke twice that season—once in the ACC Tournament?

"Beating Duke is what my fans want most," said Mark Turgeon, who was in his second season as Maryland's coach. "This is a big deal."

The Terrapins lost the next day to North Carolina and went to the NIT. But at least their fans were happy.

Miami beat North Carolina to win the ACC Tournament and went to the East Regional as a No. 2 seed. The Hurricanes reached the round of 16 before losing to Marquette. The Tar Heels went to the South Regional as a No. 8 seed and lost in the round of 32—still euphemistically called the "third" round by the NCAA—to top-seeded Kansas.

Duke was the No. 2 seed in the Midwest, behind Louisville. The regional was played in Indianapolis at Lucas Oil Stadium, the site of Duke's 2010 national championship victory. The Blue Devils managed to beat Michigan State in the round of 16, causing Spartans' coach Tom Izzo to deliver one of his more memorable lines.

"Bad enough I lose to Mike [Krzyzewski] again," he said. "But before the game, my [twelve-year-old] son Steven told me he's a Duke fan."

Izzo survived, and Steven later became a walk-on for Michigan State.

Duke did not survive, however, the regional final against Louisville. The game was close for a half, with the Cardinals leading 35–32 at the break. But the second half was a blowout that saw Louisville outscore Duke 50–31 to win the game 85–63.

Louisville went on to win the national championship but became the first school *ever* to have its national title vacated by the NCAA.

Mason Plumlee and Seth Curry, Duke's two leading scorers, graduated, as did Ryan Kelly. There was help on the way, though: Rodney Hood, a 6-8 transfer from Mississippi State; Matt Jones, a hard-nosed swingman from Texas; and Semi Ojeleye, a 6-6 forward whose parents had immigrated to Overland, Kansas, when he was very young.

But the crown jewel of the recruiting class was Jabari Parker, who had come out of the legendary Simeon High School program in Chicago and had chosen Duke over Michigan State, much to Izzo's dismay. "Honestly, I thought we had the kid," he said at the time.

Parker was 6-8 and 240 pounds and could play both inside and outside. He was a lock one-and-done and part of, along with Kentucky's Julius Randle and Kansas's Joel Embiid, what some consider to be the greatest freshmen trio in college basketball history.

In fact, after all three had played in the Champions Classic in November, ESPN's Michael Wilbon declared it "the greatest regular season night in the history of college basketball."

Not that anyone at ESPN ever resorts to hyperbole.

Parker and Hood both had excellent numbers throughout the regular season. Parker averaged more than 20 points and eight rebounds per game, and Hood averaged 16 points per game.

There was just one problem, and it was a big one: neither player could, in the immortal words of Bob Knight, guard the floor.

Duke lost two preconference games to very good teams: Kansas—in the Champions Classic on the greatest regular-season night in college basketball history—and Arizona in late December.

The season changed dramatically in December, but not because of anything that happened on the court. Mike Krzyzewski's older brother, Bill, had been diagnosed with cancer in the fall, and doctors had recommended surgery just prior to Christmas. The surgery appeared to have gone well, but the day after Christmas, Bill Krzyzewski died at the age of seventy-two.

Bill had been a fire captain in Chicago and was someone Mike had always looked up to, especially after the death of their father while Mike was in college. Bill's death shook Mike badly, and he readily admitted he wasn't the same coach for the rest of that season.

"It wasn't the kind of thing he could just put behind him," Mickie

Krzyzewski said. "He was mourning, and he couldn't just say, 'Okay, time for practice,' and move on every day. He was in shock."

Krzyzewski publicly blamed himself for his team's struggles, which included a conference season-opening loss at Notre Dame and an early loss at Clemson. They survived a home game against Virginia when a Rasheed Sulaimon three-pointer hit the rim twice and went in during the closing seconds.

Duke split with North Carolina, winning the season finale at home to finish 13–5, good enough to tie the Tar Heels for third place in what had become an overgrown fifteen-team conference. By then, Tony Bennett had built a power at Virginia, and the Cavaliers won the regular-season title with a 16–2 record.

Syracuse finished in second place, even though coach Jim Boeheim's disgust with his school's move to the ACC was very apparent, especially when Boeheim blasted Greensboro as a conference-tournament site before the tournament began. Just to prove how much Boeheim disliked Greensboro, his team lost its first game to seventh-seeded NC State.

Duke survived an opening game against Clemson 63–62—one of those games that had many people screaming "Duke gets all the calls" yet again. On the same day, Maryland played its last ACC game, losing to Florida State.

The Terrapins, who had put themselves into an untenable financial situation by needlessly building onto their football stadium, had taken the TV money the Big Ten was willing to provide and were leaving the league after sixty years.

Conference commissioner John Swofford, always prepared to raid the Big East, brought in Louisville to take Maryland's place, adding yet another school with absolutely no ACC tradition to others like Syracuse, Pittsburgh, Miami, Notre Dame, and Boston College.

Naturally, the ACC insisted on continuing its annual tradition of honoring an "ACC Legend" at the conference tournament. This led to the comical specter of players who had *never* played in the ACC being recognized as ACC "legends." To take this embarrassment a step further, the ACC set up interviews during games with some of the "legends" in attendance, leading to moments such as Syracuse "legend" Derrick Coleman telling the gushing microphone jockey, "I remember watching the ACC Tournament from Greenville every year when I was a kid."

Greenville, South Carolina—which has never hosted an ACC Tournament—is 190 miles from Greensboro, North Carolina. But what the heck, what's a couple hundred miles among legends?

The mike jockey never missed a beat, closing with, "ACC legend Derrick Coleman ladies and gentlemen!"

Having escaped Clemson and then beaten NC State, Duke met top-seeded Virginia in the final. In another game that Krzyzewski would later insist was affected (adversely for Duke) by the "Duke gets all the calls" notion, the Cavaliers won their first ACC title since 1976, when Wally Walker had been their star and Terry Holland their coach. The loss dropped Duke to a No. 3 NCAA seed and sent the Blue Devils to the Midwest Regional, scheduled again for Indianapolis.

They never got there. Playing a first-round game in Raleigh, the Blue Devils were beaten by Mercer, the Atlantic Sun champions. The Bears had beaten Florida Gulf Coast—which had been the tournament darling a year earlier when it reached the Sweet Sixteen as a No. 15 seed—in the Atlantic Sun championship game.

Mercer was a veteran team with five senior starters, and the Bears weren't the least bit intimidated by Duke's name or history. The game was perhaps best summed up by the matchup between Jabari Parker and Mercer's Jakob Gollon. Parker was about to leave Duke to be the No. 2 pick in the NBA Draft. Gollon was a sixth-year senior who had redshirted twice with knee injuries. He was already a college graduate who would get his master's degree in May. He came into the game averaging 8.1 points per game.

But Gollon completely outplayed Parker for 40 minutes, scoring 20 points and grabbing five rebounds. Parker shot 4-of-14 from the field and looked completely off his game most of the afternoon. Rodney Hood was no better, shooting 2-of-12 from the field. Only Quinn Cook's 23 points off the bench kept the game close until the end.

Down the stretch, Mercer made all the big plays and made its free throws after getting the lead. The Bears won 78–71, then—deservedly—danced on the court. Mercer shot 55 percent from the field; Duke shot 35 percent.

Ball game.

"They were men," Krzyzewski said pointedly in his postgame press conference, the clear implication being that his players had not been men. "They dug down at the end of the game and made all the plays they had to make."

As is always the case during a season-ending press conference, Krzyzewski was asked what he thought about the following season.

He laughed. "I don't even know who is going to be on my team next season, so it's hard for me to say what my team is going to look like or how it might play."

. . . .

Actually, Krzyzewski had a very good idea who was going to be on his team in 2014–15. Andre Dawkins and Tyler Thornton were graduating, and Parker and Hood were heading for the NBA Draft. Four freshmen had been signed: 6-foot-10 Jahlil Okafor from Chicago; 6-6 Justise Winslow from Houston; 6-2 point guard Tyus Jones from Apple Valley, Wisconsin; and 6-4 shooting guard Grayson Allen from Jacksonville, Florida.

All were highly rated by the so-called experts, and Okafor and Winslow were considered definite one-and-dones.

John Thompson was in the Raleigh arena that afternoon, doing radio. After the game, I asked him how Jabari Parker could be expected to compete in the NBA the next season when he couldn't compete against Jakob Gollon.

Thompson laughed. "He's not ready for the NBA, but it doesn't matter," he said. "He can't go home this summer and tell his buddies he's going to be a sophomore. Guys like him don't have that option anymore."

Krzyzewski was now fully immersed in the world of one-and-dones. He had even overtaken Kentucky's John Calipari, who hadn't invented the one-and-done (as he often pointed out) but had perfected it.

"Funny thing is, my plan was to go for two years," Justise Winslow said. "The Final Four was scheduled for Houston my sophomore year, and I was thinking, 'Play in Houston as a sophomore and then turn pro.'"

Even though Winslow had no intention of staying in college for four years, it was his mother who persuaded him to go to Duke. "I really thought all along I was going to Florida," he said, laughing. "I played on a football team called the Gators, same colors as Florida. I went to [Florida coach] Billy Donovan's camp and really liked him. But at the last second, my mom came to school one day crying and talking about how much it would mean to her if I went to Duke. That's what turned it for me."

Okafor and Jones had become friends on the summer Amateur Athletic Union (AAU) circuit and made a decision in the fall of 2013 to go somewhere together. When they both announced for Duke on the same November day, Krzyzewski was well on his way to what was arguably his best recruiting class since the famous class of '82.

Allen, a talented scorer, had already committed, and Winslow made the decision to join the three of them a week later. Only Allen was *not* considered a potential one-and-done.

Even with Parker and Hood gone to the NBA, there was still returning talent, notably senior guard Quinn Cook, who willingly gave up his point-guard spot to Tyus Jones and became the starting shooting guard. Amile Jefferson had missed a season injured but was now a redshirt junior, as was "little brother" Marshall Plumlee. Rasheed Sulaimon was also a junior after an up-and-down sophomore season.

The Blue Devils were impressive early. They won at Wisconsin, beating a team that returned all its key players from a group that had reached the Final Four the previous April. They also had wins over Connecticut, Stanford, and Michigan State.

Right from the beginning, three of the freshmen—Okafor, Winslow, and Jones—were starters, along with Cook and sophomore Matt Jones (no relation to Tyus).

The Blue Devils won their first two ACC games (the schedule now called for eighteen conference games after all the expansion) and then got blown out at NC State. That wasn't a shock, but losing to Miami 90–74 *at home* was. State and Miami had one thing in common: big strong guards who could get to the basket. Jones and Cook were both 6-2 and slender, and they were getting knocked around.

That's when Krzyzewski showed the flexibility that often separated him from other great coaches. He was a man-to-man defensive coach and a motion-offense coach at the other end of the court. But he built his team each season based on his players' talents. The best example might have been Christian Laettner, who took *one* three-point shot as a freshman and then took nearly 40 percent of his shots from beyond the line, shooting 56 percent, as a senior.

"It would have been foolish to say to Christian, 'Stay inside all the time' when he had worked so hard to develop his outside shot," Krzyzewski said.

And so, after the two losses, Krzyzewski adapted. When Duke went to play at Louisville that weekend, the Blue Devils came out in a zone defense. They won in one of the toughest buildings in the country to play in as a road team.

Then they beat Pittsburgh at home, setting up a Sunday-afternoon national TV game against St. John's in Madison Square Garden. Krzyzewski had 999 victories at that point.

Dating back to Krzyzewski's playing days, the iconic building in Midtown Manhattan had played a major role in his career. His best game as a player had come in the NIT quarterfinals when he shut down South Carolina All-American John Roche, and Army upset the Gamecocks. Duke's first victory in a national tournament had come in the Garden in the 1985 preseason NIT. And his 903rd victory, making him the all-time winningest coach in college basketball history, had also come in the Garden.

This win would not come easily. Winslow was playing even though he was sick, and the Red Storm was a solid team. They led by as many as 10 points in the second half before Tyus Jones led a rally that produced a 15–1 run and a 77–68 victory. Jones finished with 22 points, while Okafor and Cook added 17 points apiece.

A key decision by Krzyzewski helped turn the game around: he inserted Marshall Plumlee to give Okafor help inside, and Plumlee's presence made Duke a much better defensive team. He contributed two points and five rebounds in 12 minutes, but his most important contributions were energy and defense.

"Most of that season, that was my role," he said. "Go in and play with a lot of energy. Rebound. Play defense. We had plenty of scorers. I didn't need to score unless I got an offensive rebound."

Duke celebrated Krzyzewski's 1,000th victory almost like a national title. There were T-shirts with "1,000 Victories" on the front and "Coach K and Still Kounting" on the back, and dozens of ex-players were there to celebrate.

"It was a great day," Krzyzewski said later. "Although, for a long time, it didn't look like such a great day. St. John's was good."

A letdown was inevitable, and it came three days later in a 77–73 loss at

Notre Dame. The Irish were very good—they would reach the Elite Eight of the NCAA Tournament—so the loss wasn't shocking.

What was shocking was the announcement a day later that Rasheed Sulaimon had been thrown off the team. In forty years as a head coach, Krzyzewski had never thrown a player off one of his teams, either at Army or at Duke.

Sulaimon was in good standing as a student; he would graduate that summer after three years at Duke. His playing time had gone down considerably since his freshman season, and he had sulked about it at times. But there had been no sign publicly that his position on the team was in jeopardy.

Later, both the Duke *Chronicle* and *Sports Illustrated* would report that Sulaimon had been investigated the previous season after two women claimed he had assaulted them. There were never any charges, nor any evidence that what had happened almost a year earlier led to his dismissal from the team.

. . . .

Duke had only nine scholarship players, and Sulaimon was still playing an important role off the bench. Now, there were only eight scholarship players.

"I remember Coach K walking into the locker room before practice the next day and saying, 'If you [expletives] listen to me, you're going to find out that eight is enough,'" Winslow said. "'We've got everything in this room to win the national championship.' Funny thing is, we believed him."

Krzyzewski went so far as to write the number 8 on the locker-room whiteboard. Then he wrote another 8, but he turned it on its side.

A sideways 8 is the mathematical sign for infinity.

"That's our potential," he said. "It's infinite."

As was often the case in Krzyzewski's career, crisis brought out the best in him—and in his team.

Two days later, they traveled to Charlottesville to play undefeated Virginia. The Cavaliers were ranked No. 2 in the nation behind also-undefeated Kentucky, which was already being touted as one of the greatest teams of all time.

The Blue Devils hit all their key three-point shots late and stunned the Cavaliers and most in the sellout crowd of 14,953 in John Paul Jones Arena, pulling away to win 69–63.

That night, eight was certainly enough.

A week later, Notre Dame came to Cameron, and Duke went on an early 43–7 run (that's not a typo) and won 90–60 (that's not a typo, either).

The next morning, Krzyzewski stopped for gas on his way home from church. The team was leaving that afternoon to face frequent road nemesis Florida State. As he got back into his car, Krzyzewski saw that he had a text from associate athletic director Jon Jackson.

"Coach," it said, "Dean Smith passed away last night."

Krzyzewski was stunned. By then, everyone knew that Smith was gravely ill, so in that sense his death wasn't shocking.

"And yet, I *was* shocked," Krzyzewski said later that day. "I guess in my mind, Dean Smith was one of those people who would never die."

A few days later, Krzyzewski was one of the few non–North Carolina people invited to a private memorial service for Smith. He wore a Carolina blue tie. "I'd bought it in Las Vegas a few years earlier," he said. "I wasn't sure why I bought it, but that day I was very glad I did."

Eight days after Smith's death, the schedule brought UNC to Cameron Indoor Stadium. Prior to the game, during a moment of silence, the players and coaches knelt in a circle, arms locked around one another. Roy Williams and Krzyzewski knelt together and locked arms as well.

It was one of those rare sports moments where rivalries and pettiness were forgotten.

Duke won a wild game 92–90 in overtime. "I know Dean would have hated the result," Krzyzewski said afterward. "But he would have loved the intensity of the game and the fellowship before the game."

Duke also beat Carolina in the Dean Dome to finish the regular season 15–3 in the league and 29–3 overall. The Blue Devils went into the ACC Tournament as the No. 2 seed behind Virginia but lost in the semifinals to Notre Dame, which went on to beat North Carolina to win the tournament.

"Notre Dame was a funny team for us that year," Marshall Plumlee said. "We either crushed them or lost to them. There was no in-between."

. . . .

With a 30–4 record, Duke was still a No. 1 seed and was sent to the NCAA South Regional, which was to be played in Houston. "I got to go home a year earlier than I expected," Justise Winslow said with a laugh.

This time, there were no first-round nightmares for Duke. The Blue Devils cruised through two games in Charlotte to give Winslow his homecoming. He paid his teammates back in spades, scoring 21 points and getting 16 rebounds in a tough Sweet Sixteen game against Utah that Duke won 63–57. He then scored 16 points in the regional finals against second-seeded Gonzaga and was co–high scorer, along with Matt Jones, in Duke's 66–52 victory.

That score was deceiving. Duke trailed early in the second half and led 52–50 when Gonzaga's Kyle Wiltjer (a Kentucky transfer) missed a layup with just under five minutes to play. That miss seemed to take the life out of Gonzaga. Winslow hit a three, Matt Jones hit a three, and Tyus Jones made a steal that led to an Okafor layup. The Blue Devils outscored the Zags 14–2 to pull away and reach Krzyzewski's twelfth Final Four.

The key to the game and to the regional was Duke's defense. Krzyzewski had spent most of February gradually returning to man-to-man defense, using the zone when his team needed a defensive break or in case of foul trouble. By the time March rolled around—with the exception of the Notre Dame game in the ACC Tournament—Duke had become an excellent defensive team.

"The funny thing is, I thought our biggest problem in January was our offense," Krzyzewski said. "Sometimes, bad offense leads to bad defense. You give up easy shots off your own poor shots or turnovers. Remember, we had three freshman starters. They were talented but they were learning as they went.

"Playing zone took some mental pressure off them on offense as well as defense. Gradually, we were able to get back to man-to-man as our primary defense, and we were a lot more confident—and a lot better—in it when we did."

Three No. 1 seeds had reached the Final Four: Duke, Wisconsin, and 38–0 Kentucky. The Wildcats had looked vulnerable, though, needing to come from behind late to beat Notre Dame 68–66 in their regional final. Wisconsin had beaten Arizona in the West Regional final and was spoiling to play Kentucky. The Wildcats had beaten the Badgers at the buzzer in the 2014 Final Four.

Duke's opponent in the opening game in Indianapolis would be Michigan State. The Spartans had gotten "Izzo-hot" in March, reaching the Final Four for the seventh time under coach Tom Izzo. They had entered the tournament with ten losses as a No. 7 seed and, for the second year in a row, had upset Virginia, this time in the second round. Villanova, the No. 1 seed in the East, was also upset in the second round, losing to No. 8 seed North Carolina State. The Spartans went on to Syracuse, where they beat Oklahoma and then won a dramatic overtime game against Louisville to reach another Final Four.

Because Kentucky's bid to become the first unbeaten team since Indiana in 1976 had become such a massive story, the Wildcats and Badgers were assigned the second Saturday night game by CBS/TNT. It was the first time since 1990 in Denver—eight Duke Final Fours ago—that the Blue Devils had gotten to play the first game.

"It had been so long that I'd forgotten what an advantage it is to play first," Krzyzewski said later. "You get to bed before midnight."

Michigan State jumped to a 14–6 lead, Denzel Valentine making three quick three-point shots. But that was pretty much it for the Spartans. Even with Winslow in foul trouble, Duke dominated the rest of the half, outscoring Michigan State 30–11 to lead 36–25 at the break. Grayson Allen came off the bench to make back-to-back drives, including a massive dunk, to help spark his team.

"People still don't know how good Grayson is and how good he's going to be," Krzyzewski said afterward. "He's gotten better and better in the last two months."

Krzyzewski didn't know it at the time, but his comments turned out to be an important harbinger.

The closest Michigan State got in the second half was 44–31. Allen again provided an offensive spark, dunking his own miss on the next possession, and the Blue Devils pulled away to win 81–61. Winslow ended up with 19 points and nine rebounds, and Okafor, who was excellent in the first half, finished with 18 points. Allen had nine in 17 minutes.

But the key, again, was the defense. After the Spartans made four threes in the first five minutes, they shot 3-of-20 for the rest of the first half. After making 4-of-5 shots to start the game, Michigan State was 18-of-50 the rest of the way and 3-of-16 from three-point range.

Duke's margin was a surprise, but the outcome wasn't. Almost half the building was empty when the first game began because Kentucky fans had bought so many tickets in anticipation of their team's coronation and didn't arrive in time to see the "preliminary" game.

The coronation never happened.

After having barely lost to Kentucky a year earlier, Wisconsin was hardly intimidated by the Wildcats' aura. The game was tight throughout and tied at 36 at halftime. Wisconsin led for much of the second half, but an 8–0 Kentucky run put the Wildcats up 60–56 with under five minutes to play. It was that kind of run that had carried Kentucky through a number of tight games, including the regional final against Notre Dame.

This time, though, Kentucky's lead didn't hold up. Wisconsin's Sam Dekker made a strong drive and lay-in to make it 60–58, and after a Wildcats shot-clock violation, Nigel Hayes made a putback to tie the score with 2:39 to play.

After Andrew Harrison missed a floater, Dekker nailed a three and then took a charge. He then was fouled and made one of two free throws, and the score was—stunningly—64–60 Wisconsin with 1:06 left. The Badgers made their free throws down the stretch and won 71–64.

The silence of the thousands of Kentucky fans leaving the building was deafening. Wisconsin shot just under 48 percent against a team that had given up an average of just under 35 percent for the season. The Wildcats were called for *three* 35-second violations in the final five minutes.

"I don't think we were called for three of those all season," John Calipari said.

Badgers center Frank Kaminsky had 20 points and 11 rebounds, and Dekker had 16 points. Kentucky's all-SEC forward Willie Cauley-Stein was held to two points. Karl-Anthony Towns, who would be the No. 1 pick in the NBA Draft, had 16, but it wasn't enough.

Although Calipari tried to claim the season had been "a magic carpet ride" for people in the state of Kentucky, most people weren't buying it—including his players. "I feel like the whole season was a waste," guard Tyler Ulis said, probably summing up how most Kentucky fans felt.

Most of Duke's players were disappointed that Kentucky had lost. "We wanted to play them," Winslow said. "We'd heard all season how great they were, and we wanted a shot to play them with the championship on the line."

Instead, they got a Wisconsin team that was now convinced it was destined to be the champion. The Badgers were a better team than the one Duke had beaten in November. They were 36–3, and Hayes and Kaminsky had become the most formidable front line duo in the country. Their coach, Bo Ryan, knew how to win titles: he'd won four Division III titles at Wisconsin-Platteville and had taken Wisconsin to fourteen NCAA Tournaments in his fourteen years as the Badgers coach.

The game was tied at halftime, but with Kaminsky schooling Okafor, Wisconsin built a 48–39 lead with a little more than 12 minutes left. Okafor had four fouls and only six points at that moment. Matt Jones, Duke's fifth starter, was also struggling and hadn't scored.

Krzyzewski knew he was already deep into his bag of tricks. He decided to go deeper. He put Marshall Plumlee into the game, knowing that Plumlee couldn't possibly conjure the offense that Okafor might but that his size might slow Kaminsky down.

And he put Grayson Allen back into the game. Allen was the team's oft-forgotten freshman. He had been highly recruited and was the first player in the class to commit to Duke, doing so as a junior. He had watched Duke's national championship victory over Butler in 2010 and had thought to himself, "It would be fun to play for them."

Now, in another national championship game in the same building, Krzyzewski sent Allen back into the game looking for some energy—and some points.

"At that point, I was out of ideas," he said. "They'd outplayed us, and Bo had outcoached me. If Grayson hadn't done what he did, I had nothing left."

What Allen did was simple: he turned the game around. With the score 48–39, he drilled a three-pointer. Then, on what his teammates later called the most memorable play of the game, he dove on a loose ball, made the steal, and hit another three. He was then fouled after getting an offensive rebound. His two free throws made the score 48–46.

"Honestly, of all my memories of that night, Grayson on that loose ball is the most vivid," Winslow said. "He and Marshall were the reasons we won the game. Not that Tyus [Jones] and Jahlil [Okafor] and Quinn [Cook] didn't do a lot, but we don't win without those two guys."

Jon Scheyer, then an assistant coach, agreed. "Until Coach K put those two guys in, we were dead in the water," he said.

Plumlee played nine minutes during Duke's rally—the Blue Devils finished the game on a 29–15 run—and didn't score. But his defense and his enthusiasm were enough to slow down Wisconsin and, with Allen's spurt, turn the game around. He also became the third Plumlee brother to win a national title at Duke. This from a player who had almost gone to Virginia, thinking he would get more playing time there.

Two months later, sitting in his office, Krzyzewski got emotional talking about Plumlee and Allen.

"Marshall was one of those guys who did everything you ever asked, every day," Krzyzewski said. "He was the epitome of the guy who, when you said 'stay ready,' he did exactly that. When we needed him in the most important game of the season, he was ready. Completely ready."

And Allen?

Krzyzewski was silent for a moment. "You know, I've had a lot of great players do a lot of great things," he said. "But no one's ever done anything quite like Grayson that night. He had to wait half a season to really get his chance. Even then, his minutes were up and down.

"What he did, coming in and giving us that burst . . . well, it was unbelievable. Just unbelievable."

Allen finished with 16 points in 21 minutes. In the final few minutes, Okafor—refreshed from his stint on the bench—hit two key baskets, and Tyus Jones hit two critical three-pointers. He then hit the last two free throws of the game to extend Duke's margin to 68–63 after Wisconsin had closed the lead to three in the final seconds.

Early in the season, a Duke blogger who watched every minute of every game had nicknamed Jones "Stones" because he always seemed to make big plays at critical moments. "Stones" finished with 23 points and was voted the Most Outstanding Player of the Final Four.

The final score was 68–63, and Krzyzewski confirmed what everybody now knew when it was over. "As it turned out," he said, "eight *was* enough."

When the team returned to Cameron the next day to be greeted by the student body, Krzyzewski didn't have to ask where to put banner number five. It would go right next to banners one, two, three, and four.

Where once there were none, now there are five.

Epilogue

On the night of November 7, 2022, Jon Scheyer walked onto the court at Cameron Indoor Stadium, something he had done hundreds of times since the fall of 2006. "The place where I grew up," he said later about Duke's home venue.

This time, though, was different.

Scheyer had jogged onto the court as a Duke player for four years, and he had walked onto it as a Duke assistant coach and as Mike Krzyzewski's associate head coach for eight years.

Now, though, the entire building awaited his entrance. He was about to become the first person in forty-two years to start a season as the new Duke men's head basketball coach.

As Scheyer came onto the floor and walked toward the bench, intentionally taking an indirect route that allowed him to exchange palm slaps with many of the students, the chant began: "We want six! We want six!"

Scheyer was unaware of the chant; he was completely in the moment, savoring the fact that he was now Duke's head coach, successor to the iconic Krzyzewski, while also wondering nervously how his team would play.

"I didn't hear it," he said, laughing, when the game was over and Duke had beaten Jacksonville University easily. "But I can certainly believe it."

Part of Krzyzewski's legacy is that he left the Cameron rafters stuffed with banners: twenty-two ACC Tournament championship banners, fifteen won by Krzyzewski; seventeen Final Four banners, thirteen earned by Krzyzewski; and a banner that hangs at the south end commemorating Krzyzewski's NCAA record 1,202 victories.

But the five banners that matter most, the ones the students were chanting to increase to six, hang at the north end of Cameron. They all say "National Champions" on them, and they all were won by Krzyzewski's teams.

Scheyer is expected to add a sixth at some point in the not-too-distant future. So much for reasonable expectations.

"I understood that when I took the job," Scheyer said. "Coach K set an unbelievably high bar, and all I can do is try the best I can to come somewhere close to it."

....

The last of the five banners was hung in 2015, after the "Eight Is Enough" national championship in Indianapolis. Three of the five starters from that team—Jahlil Okafor, Justise Winslow, and Tyus Jones—left Duke after one season, but only after Krzyzewski insisted they at least finish the spring semester academically.

"I knew they weren't going to graduate," he said. "But I didn't want them to leave before they at least finished one year."

The next seven seasons didn't produce another national championship; in fact, most of Duke's numbers went down. The overall record of 183–55 would have pleased about 99 percent of the schools in the country, but an average season of 26–8 was not up to standards—specifically, Krzyzewski's standards. After winning the ACC Tournament eleven times in seventeen seasons, there were only two ACC Tournament titles: one in 2017 and the other in 2019. After eleven regular-season titles in twenty seasons, there were none for eleven straight seasons beginning in 2010–11. After twelve Final Fours in thirty seasons, there were none for Duke from 2016 through 2021.

Duke was good, just not great. The "one-and-dones" continued to swirl through the revolving door—some, like Jayson Tatum and Brandon Ingram, going on to NBA stardom, and others, like Zion Williamson, having immense talent but carrying a "perennially injured" asterisk.

Duke reached the Elite Eight in 2018, losing in overtime to Kansas after a Grayson Allen jumper that would have won the game went in and out at the buzzer in regulation. A year later, the Blue Devils were stunned by Michigan State in the regional final, losing 68–67. That was Duke's so-called super team, led by three one-and-dones: Williamson, Cam Reddish, and R. J. Barrett.

The Blue Devils were actually lucky to make the Elite Eight that year. Only a missed follow by Johnny Dawkins's son Aubrey allowed them to beat the University of Central Florida (UCF), coached by Dawkins, and another missed layup at the buzzer allowed them to escape Virginia Tech in the round of 16.

The night before the regional final, I had dinner with Tom Izzo. "You can beat them," I told him. "You're tougher than they are. They think they'll always find a way to win because they're so talented. I think you win tomorrow."

In this case, I was right. The Spartans made plays down the stretch and Duke didn't.

"You were right," Izzo said to me after the game. He smiled and added, "For once."

That evening was the first time Krzyzewski sounded worn out to me after a loss. He said all the right things, but there was strain in his voice and exhaustion on his face. It was the first time the thought occurred to me that the end was near.

It might have come in 2021, but Duke had its worst season since Krzyzewski's "lost season" in 1995. The Blue Devils were 13–11 and barely hanging on to the NCAA Tournament bubble when a positive test for COVID-19 forced them to forfeit their ACC quarterfinal game to Florida State, ending their season without an NCAA Tournament bid for the first time since 1995—not counting the non-tournament season of 2020, when Duke was 25–6 before COVID shut everything down.

Krzyzewski didn't want his career to end on such a down note. But he was ready. On June 2, 2021, he announced he would retire at the end of the 2022 season and that Scheyer would succeed him. The other finalist for the job was Harvard coach Tommy Amaker, who was, like Scheyer, a great Krzyzewski point guard.

Many thought it was well past time for Duke to hire a Black coach, even though there hadn't been an opening for a head basketball coach at Duke since 1980. Amaker had been hugely successful at Harvard and, unlike Scheyer, had head coaching experience. Scheyer had the advantage of having been part of the program for most of the previous sixteen years and also being twenty-two years younger than Amaker.

Many people wondered why Krzyzewski didn't wait until season's end to announce he was retiring. "I had to do it for recruiting," he explained. "I couldn't go into kids' homes in September and have them say, 'How much longer are you going to coach?,' and either lie or tell the truth. I couldn't lie, and the truth would have been public instantly. This way, Jon had a clear shot at his own recruiting class."

....

Krzyzewski's final season ended on a sour note but was at times filled with joy. The Blue Devils won thirty-two games and the ACC regular-season title. The regular-season finale was a huge disappointment: Carolina, now coached by Hubert Davis, came into Cameron and outplayed the Blue Devils in the second half, avenging a loss a month earlier in the Dean Dome.

The Tar Heels danced on the court. They had earned it.

Duke reached the ACC final before losing to Virginia Tech and was sent to the West Regional as the No. 2 seed behind Gonzaga. One could feel the stifling pressure every time they took the court.

"We all felt the 'this could be Coach K's last game' pressure," Scheyer said. "The kids did a great job handling it."

In the second round, Krzyzewski faced his old friend Izzo one last time. Michigan State led for much of the game, but Duke rallied for an 85–76 victory.

"I thought we had 'em," Izzo said afterward. "This time, they were tougher than us. They deserved the win."

The regionals were in San Francisco—not Anaheim, which had been a house of horrors for Duke through the years—and the Blue Devils beat Texas Tech and Arkansas, which had upset Gonzaga in the round of 16.

And so, in his final season, Krzyzewski set one last record: he made a thirteenth Final Four, one more than John Wooden.

North Carolina had also made the Final Four, and for the first time ever, the two teams would meet in the NCAA Tournament—thirty-two years after both had played in the 1991 Final Four. This time, the outcome wasn't as happy for Duke as it had been then.

Whether it was the pressure of Duke-Carolina with the world watching, the stress of this possibly being Coach K's last game, or just that the Tar Heels were the better team, Carolina won an extremely tight semifinal game 81–77.

It was a thud ending to a wonderful season for Duke. Carolina looked like it was going to win the national championship when it led Kansas by 15 points at halftime on Monday night, but the Jayhawks rallied to win the title.

They had beaten Villanova in the semifinals on Saturday in what was, as it turned out, Jay Wright's last game after a Hall of Fame coaching career on the Philadelphia Main Line. He announced his retirement eighteen days after the loss to Kansas.

"I had a pretty good career," he said, laughing. "And then, I was only the second-best coach to retire at that Final Four."

Scheyer had an excellent first season following his mentor. Duke beat North Carolina twice—hardly revenge for what had happened the previous season, but satisfying nonetheless—and won the ACC Tournament, beating Virginia in the final.

As a No. 5 seed in the East Regional, the Blue Devils were woefully underseeded in the NCAA Tournament; perhaps the committee believed Duke had stopped playing the same level of basketball after Krzyzewski retired. They were soundly beaten in the second round by fourth-seeded Tennessee, which was bigger, stronger, and more experienced and pulled away late. It was just a bad matchup for Duke.

Even with the loss, the Blue Devils finished 27–9, and it is clear that Duke is in good hands with Scheyer as coach.

National championship banner number six is a lofty—but not unreasonable—expectation.

. . . .

The day after Scheyer made his debut, I went to meet Krzyzewski and our mutual friend Keith Drum for lunch at the Washington Duke Inn, which is directly across from a main entrance to Duke's West Campus.

I didn't know if Mike and Keith had arrived yet, so I said to the maître d' that I was meeting Mike Krzyzewski, figuring he'd know if he was already there. I was greeted with a blank look.

"Do you have a reservation?" he asked.

Before I could answer, the manager walked up, shaking his head and saying, "I haven't seen Coach K today." I'm pretty sure he was about to add "and who the hell are you?" when Krzyzewski and Drum walked in. Now the maître d' was looking at all three of us blankly.

I couldn't resist.

"Hey Mike, you haven't been the coach for one game and they've already forgotten you," I said.

Krzyzewski smiled. "I think I'll be okay," he said.

Indeed.

Index

Buckley, Clay, 58
Buckner, Quinn, 51
Burgess, Chris, 100
Burrell, Scott, 24
Butler University: 2000–2001 games, 108; 2002–3 games, 128; in 2010 NCAA Tournament, 146–50, 174, *12–13*; 2010–11 games, 156; in 2011 NCAA Tournament, 158
Butters, Tom, 3–4, 7, 11–12, 21, 88, 91–92, 135
Byers, Walter, 29
Bynum, Will, 133
Byrd, Rick, 139

Calhoun, Jim, 24, 25, 102, 133, 134, 158
California (University of, at Berkeley), 84
California (University of, at Los Angeles) (UCLA): 1964 Duke game, 58; in 1968 NCAA Tournament, 29–30; 1973 title, 39, 44; in 1990 NCAA Tournament, 24, 25, 46; 1991–92 games, 65, 76; in 1992 NCAA Tournament, 74; in 2001 NCAA Tournament, 113, 114; 2002–3 games, 128; in 2006 NCAA Tournament, 137; Wooden as coach at, 29, 44, 51
Calipari, John, 166, 173
Cameron Crazies, 8–9
Cameron Indoor Stadium, 1; championship banners hung in, 58, 82, *16*; record of North Carolina in, 61; student section in, 8–9
Capel, Jeff, 86, 87, 89, 96
Carlesimo, P. J., 66
Carrawell, Chris: in 1996–97 season, 95, 96–97; in 1997–98 season, 100; in 1998–99 season, 101; in 1999–2000 season, 103, 104, 107; graduation of, 107
Carrier Dome, 40
Cauley-Stein, Willie, 173
CBS: 1989 postgame interview on, 21; and 1991 NCAA probation of UNLV, 58–59; 1991 NCAA Tournament on, 36, 41, 54; 1991 Packer Points pregame show on, 45; 1992 Duke vs. Kentucky game on, 70; 1994

NCAA Tournament games on, 87, 93; 2001 NCAA Tournament games on, 113; 2011 contract on NCAA Tournaments, 153, 155; 2015 NCAA Tournament games on, 172
Central Florida (University of), 6, 179
Champions Classic, 159, 163
Charles, Lorenzo, 10–11
Charlotte Coliseum, 40, 87
Charlotte Observer, 120
Cheaney, Calbert, 74, 78
Chicago Tribune, 103
Chilcutt, Pete, 32, 35, 41, 46
Childress, Randolph, 64
Christensen, Matt, 110, 111
Chronicle, 2, 8, 169
Cincinnati (University of), 73, 76, 101
Clark, Marty: in 1990–91 season, 32, 39, 43, 52; in 1991–92 season, 58; in 1993–94 season, 86; graduation of, 89
Clemson University: 1983–84 games, 12; 1989–90 games, 23, 24–25; in 1995 ACC Tournament, 90; 2013–14 games, 164, 165; Barnes as coach at, 62
Cleveland Cavaliers, 6
Clinton, Bill, 88
Coach K. *See* Krzyzewski, Mike
Cole Field House, 108, 109
Coleman, Derrick, 37, 164–65
Collins, Chris, 86, 88, 89, 94, 149, *11*
Colorado (University of), 98–99
Connecticut (University of): in 1990 NCAA Tournament, 24, 25–27; in 1991 NCAA Tournament, 37; 1994–95 season, 90; in 1999 NCAA Tournament, 102–3; 1999–2000 games, 104; in 2004 NCAA Tournament, 133–34, 146; in 2011 NCAA Tournament, 158; 2014–15 games, 167
Cook, Anthony, 19
Cook, Quinn, 159, 165, 167, 168, 175, *14, 15*
Corchiani, Chris, 34
Corrigan, Gene, 55, 56
Cousins, DeMarcus, 144
COVID-19 pandemic, 53, 179
Cragg, Mike, 156–57

Lang, Antonio: in 1991–92 season, 58, 64, 65, 67, 76; in 1992 NCAA Tournament, 76; in 1993–94 season, 86, 87; in 1994 NCAA Tournament, 88; graduation of, 89

Langdon, Trajan, 89, 95, 96, 100, 103

Larrañaga, Jim, 162

LaSalle University, 67

Leary, Todd, 76

Lebo, Jeff, 17

Ledford, Cawood, 72–73

Lehigh University, 160–61

"Lethal Weapon 3" team of Georgia Tech, 23, 34

Lewis, Michael, 112

Livingston, Shaun, 135

Lofton, Kenny, 19

Long Beach State University, 28, 29

Los Angeles Lakers, 135

Louisiana State University, 63, 64, 137

Louisville (University of): 1980 championship, 142, 150; in 1983 NCAA Tournament, 27; 1985–86 games, 16, 28, 58, 59–60; 2012–13 games, 162; 2014–15 games, 168, 172; NCAA violations, 162; Smith (Derek) as player at, 142, 150

Love, Reggie, 110, 111

Lowe, Sidney, 10

Loyola Marymount University, 28

Lucas, D. Wayne, 95

Lucas, Kalin, 145

Lucas Oil Stadium, 146, 150, 12

Lucious, Korie, 145

Lundquist, Verne, 70

Lupica, Mike, 26, 55, 59–60

Lynch, George, 32, 63, 84, 85

Mack, Shelvin, 148

Macon, Mark, 37

Madison Square Garden games: in 1985–86 season, 14, 168; in 1996–97 season, 95; in 1999–2000 season, 104; in 2000–2001 season, 108; in 2007–8 season, 138; in 2011–12 season, 159; in 2014–15 season, 168

Maggette, Corey, 101, 103

Majerus, Rick, 101

Manning, Danny, 16

Market Square Arena, 40, 150

Marquette University, 87, 93–94, 162

Maryland (University of): 1972–73 games, 1; 1983–84 games, 8, 12, 13; 1984–85 games, 14; 1990–91 games, 34; 1991–92 games, 63, 64, 65; 1994–95 games, 92, 109; 1996–97 games, 94, 95–96, 97; 1999–2000 games, 104, 108; 2000–2001 games, 108–9, 110, 111; in 2001 ACC Tournament, 112; in 2001 NCAA Tournament, 112–13, 114–17, 118, 124; 2001–2 games, 124, 125; in 2002 NCAA Tournament, 125, 128; 2002–3 games, 128; in 2004 ACC Tournament, 132–33, 134; 2006–7 games, 138; 2009–10 games, 144, 145; 2012–13 games, 162; in 2014 ACC Tournament, 164; NCAA sanctions against, 108; officiating complaints of, 117

Mashburn, Jamal, 68, 69, 70

Massachusetts (University of), 94–95

Maui, tournament games in, 124, 160

Maynor, Eric, 138

Mazzulla, Joe, 139

McCaffrey, Billy, 22, 39, 53, 54

McCollum, C. J., 161

McGeachy, Neill, 2, 5

McGuire, Al, 19–20, 26, 50, 73

McInnis, Jeff, 85

McLeod, Roshown, 100

McRoberts, Josh, 136, 138

Meadowlands: 1986 games in, 15; 1989 games in, 19, 20, 21; 1990 games in, 24; 1991 games in, 36, 37; 1996 games in, 40; 2010 games in, 156

Meek, Erik, 58, 89

Meeks, Jamal, 76

Melchionni, Gary, 1

Memphis State University, 44

Memphis (University of), 14

Mercer University, 165

Miami Heat, 89

Miami (University of), 138, 160, 162, 167

one-and-done players, 136, 140–41, 167, 178, 179; Irving as, 144, 155; Krzyzewski immersed in, 166; Krzyzewski resistance to, 136, 140, 141; Okafor as, 166; Parker as, 163; Rivers as, 159; Williams (Marvin) as, 136; Winslow as, 166
O'Toole, Tim, 93
Owens, Billy, 37
Owens, Trelonnie, 64

Packer, Billy, 45, 49, 54, 56, 104
Palmer, Crawford, 19
Parker, Jabari: in 2013–14 season, 163, 165, *14*; in NBA, 165, 166, 167
Parks, Cherokee: in 1991–92 season, 58, 65, 75; in 1992–93 season, 84; in 1993–94 season, 86, 88; in 1994–95 season, 89
Patriot League, 160–61
Patsos, Jimmy, 132
Paulus, Greg, 136, 138, 142
Pavia, Pete, 46, 47; call against Bilas (1986), 16, 46, 52, 60; cancer diagnosis of, 16, 46
Pelphrey, John, 68, 70, 71
Penders, Tom, 156
Pennsylvania State University, 37, 113
Pepperdine University, 14
Peppers, Julius, *7*
Perkins, Sam, 8, 9, 60
Phelps, Derrick, 32, 35, 63, 84
Phelps, Digger, 125
Philadelphia Daily News, 28
Pierce, Charlie, 59
Pitino, Rick: and 1992 Duke vs. Kentucky game, 67–72; and 1994 NCAA Tournament, 86–87
Pittsburgh (University of), 138, 168
Plumlee, Marshall, 159, 167, 168, 170, 174, 175
Plumlee, Mason, 143, 156, 159, 161, 163
Plumlee, Miles, 140, 143, 156, 159
Portland Trail Blazers, 89, 157
Price, Ricky, 89
Princeton University, 113
Providence College, 67, 98
Purdue University, 87, 132, 146

race, as issue, 29, 59–61, 99; in Texas Western vs. Kentucky game (1966), 2, 60, 99
Rainbow Classic (Hawaii), 90
Randall, Mark, 53
Randle, Julius, 163
Randolph, Shavlik, 128, 129, 131–32, 133
recruitment of players: by Foster, 5–6; of Hill, 32; Kansas violations in, 39, 46, 53; by Kentucky, 29, 68; by Krzyzewski, 6, 58, 100, 103, 136, 140–41, 144, 155, 161; of Laettner, 42; by Smith, 17, 84, 101; by Tarkanian, 29
Reddish, Cam, 179
Redick, J. J., 128, 129, 131, 134, 136, 137, *9*
Reed, Neil, 125
Reese, Brian, 32, 84
Reid, J. R., 17
Reynolds, Chris, 74
Reynolds Coliseum, 94
Rice, King, 32, 35, 46
Richardson, Nolan, 27
Richmond (University of), 37
Rivers, Austin, 159, 160, 161
Robinson, David, 15, 16
Robinson, Glenn, 87
Robinson, Les, 94
Roche, John, 79, 168
Roe, Delvon, 145
Rogers, Rodney, 64
Rogers, Tom, 77, 78
Rozier, Clifford, 32
Rupp, Adolph, 1–2, 98, 99, 120, 150
Rupp Arena, 125
Russell, Bill, 60
Ryan, Bo, 174

Saint John's University: in 1985 NCAA Tournament, 28; 1985–86 games, 14; 1989–90 games, 24; in 1991 NCAA Tournament, 37–38; 1999–2000 games, 104; 2014–15 games, 168
Saint Joseph's University, 133
Salvadori, Kevin, 84
Sampson, Ralph, 7, 8

San Antonio Spurs, 46
Sanders, Casey, 110, 111, 114
Sanford, Terry, 8
Schaap, Dick, 26
Scheyer, Jon: in 2006–7 season, 137, 141; in
  2008–9 season, 142, 143; in 2009–10 sea-
  son, 143, 144–45; in 2010 NCAA Tour-
  nament, 146, 147, 149, 150, 151, 157, 12; as
  assistant coach, 175, 180; graduation of,
  156; as head coach, 177–78, 179–80, 181
Scott, Dennis, 23, 24
Scott, Richard, 46
Self, Bill, 53
Sendek, Herb, 97
Senior Night games, 6, 23, 65, 110, 137, 144
Seton Hall University, 22, 45, 66–67, 103
Shaheen, Greg, 154–55
Shalin, Mike, 113
Singler, Kyle: in 2007–8 season, 138; in
  2008–9 season, 140, 143; in 2009–10 season, 143, 144; in 2010 NCAA Tournament,
  146, 147, 148, 149; in 2010–11 season, 156;
  in NBA, 157
Smith, Dean: and 1974 "eight-points-in-17-
  seconds" game, 2; and 1977 NCAA Tournament, 28; 1983–84 season, 8–9, 10;
  1987–88 season, 18; 1988–89 season,
  20–21; and 1991 NCAA Tournament, 37, 38,
  39, 45–48; and 1993 national championship, 83; 1993–94 season, 85; 1994–95 season, 92; 1996–97 season, 96, 97, 98, 99; in
  Basketball Hall of Fame, 29, 43; competitive personality of, 19; and Dean Dome,
  14–15, 61, 62; death of, 170; and double-
  standard game vs. Duke, 10, 61; number
  of Final Four games, 133, 146; recruitment
  of players by, 17, 84, 101; retirement of,
  99–100; and Williams, 110; winning record of, 121, 156
Smith, Derek, 142
Smith, John, 2
Smith, Kenny, 8, 17
Smith, Nolan: in 2007–8 season, 138; in
  2008–9 season, 140, 142–43; in 2009–10

season, 143, 144, 145; in 2010 NCAA Tour-
  nament, 146, 147, 148, 150; in 2010–11 sea-
  son, 156, 157–58; in NBA, 157
Smith, Sam, 103
Smith, Tony, 86
Snyder, Quin, 17, 19, 21–22, 93, 103, 113, 2
Solomon, George, 2
South Carolina State University, 90
South Carolina (University of), 3
Southern California (University of), 114
Southern Illinois University, 84
Southwest Missouri State University, 102
Spanarkel, Jim, 3, 6, 60
Spectrum Arena, 66, 113, 4
Sports Illustrated, 74, 97, 169
The Sports Reporters (TV show), 26
Stackhouse, Jerry, 85
Stanford University, 98, 104, 108, 113, 167
Stern, David, 89
Stevens, Brad, 147, 148
Stockton, Dick, 26–27
Strickland, Kevin, 17, 2
Sulaimon, Rasheed, 161, 164, 167, 169
Sullivan, Pat, 84
Superdome, 45
Sutton, Eddie, 68
Swofford, John, 164
Syracuse University, 15, 37, 129, 146, 164

Tar Heel Sports Network, 63
Tarkanian, Jerry, 28–29, 49, 50, 59
Tatum, Jayson, 178
Taylor, Dean, 139
Temple, Garrett, 137
Temple University, 18, 37, 102, 160
Tennessee (University of), 181
Texas Southern University, 86
Texas Tech University, 94, 159, 180
Texas (University of), 137, 140
Texas Western University vs. Kentucky
  (1966), 2, 60, 99
Thomas, Lance, 137, 143, 144, 156, 157
Thomas, Tyrus, 137